The Norton Scores

TENTH EDITION
VOLUME I

TENTH EDITION
IN TWO VOLUMES

The Norton Scores
A Study Anthology

Volume I: Gregorian Chant to Beethoven

edited by
Kristine Forney
PROFESSOR OF MUSIC, CALIFORNIA STATE UNIVERSITY, LONG BEACH

with textual notes by
Roger Hickman
PROFESSOR OF MUSIC, CALIFORNIA STATE UNIVERSITY, LONG BEACH

W. W. NORTON & COMPANY
NEW YORK ✄ LONDON

Copyright © 2007, 2003, 1999, 1995, 1990, 1984, 1977, 1970, 1968 by W. W. Norton &
Company, Inc.

Composition by GGS Book Services
Manufacturing by Victor Graphics
Book design by: Antonina Krass and David Budmen

ISBN 13: 978-0-393-92889-1 (pbk.)
ISBN 10: 0-393-92889-6 (pbk.)

W. W. Norton & Company, Inc., 500 Fifth Avenue, New York, N.Y. 10110
www.wwnorton.com

W. W. Norton & Company Ltd., Castle House, 75/76 Wells Street, London W1T 3QT

1 2 3 4 5 6 7 8 9 0

Contents

Preface

The Tenth Edition of *The Norton Scores* provides a comprehensive approach to the study of the masterworks of Western music literature, from the earliest times to the present. Published in two volumes, the anthology serves several teaching and study roles in the field of music, including the following:

- as a core anthology, or an ancillary, for a masterworks-oriented music class, to aid in the development of listening and music-reading skills;
- as a study anthology for a music history class focused on major repertory, genres, or styles of Western music;
- as a core repertory for analysis classes, providing a wide variety of styles, forms, and genres;
- as a central text for a capstone course in musical styles focused on standard repertory, listening, or score study;
- as an ancillary to a beginning conducting course and a help in reading full orchestral scores;
- as an independent study resource for those wishing to expand their knowledge of repertory and styles;
- as a resource for music teachers in a wide array of courses.

The Norton Scores can be used independently, as described above, or in conjunction with an introductory music text. The repertory coordinates with *The Enjoyment of Music*, Tenth Edition, by Kristine Forney and Joseph Machlis. Recording packages are available for use with this edition: 8 CDs (in two volumes matching the contents and division of the score volumes) and 4 CDs (selected works).

The anthology presents many works in their entirety; others are represented by one or more movements or an excerpt. Most selections are reproduced in full scores; however, opera excerpts are given in piano/vocal scores. (In the case of some contemporary pieces, issues of copyright and practicality prevent the inclusion of a complete score.) Translations are provided for all foreign-texted vocal works, and each score is followed by an informative text that provides historical and stylistic information about the work.

The full scores in this anthology employ a unique system of highlighting that directs students who are just developing music-reading skills to pre-selected elements in the score, thus enhancing the music-listening experience. Students with good music-reading skills will, of course, perceive many additional details. Each system (or group of staves) is covered with a light gray screen, within which the most prominent musical lines are highlighted with white bands. Where two or more simultaneous musical lines are equally prominent, they are both highlighted. Multiple musical systems on a page are separated by a thin white band. For more information, see "How to Follow the Highlighted Scores" on p. xii. This highlighting system has been applied to most instrumental works in full scores; in vocal works, the text generally serves as a guide throughout the work.

The highlighting is not intended as an analysis of the melodic structure, contrapuntal texture, or any other musical aspect of the work. Since it emphasizes the most prominent line (or lines), however, it often represents the principal thematic material in a work. In some cases, the highlighting may shift mid-phrase to another instrument that becomes more audible.

Here are some considerations regarding the repertory included in this anthology:

- The repertory is divided into two volumes:
  - Volume 1: Gregorian Chant to Beethoven
  - Volume 2: Schubert to the Present
  - 8-CD set matches this division
- All major Classical genres are represented:
  - Wide-ranging genres, including chant, mass, motet, chanson, madrigal (Italian and English), Italian cantata, opera, oratorio, Lied, song cycle, choral part song, piano music, sonata, dance music, chamber music, concerto, symphony, ballet suite, ragtime, blues, jazz, musical theater, other orchestral genres, traditional and world musics, and computer music.
  - New works in this edition include, in Volume 1, a troubadour dance song, ensemble dance music from the Renaissance, a Handel opera aria, a Scarlatti keyboard sonata, a French Baroque dance piece, a Classical-era trumpet concerto, and a Requiem mass; in Volume 2, a Chopin polonaise, a Gottschalk dance for piano, a Fanny Mendelssohn choral part song, a Ravel song cycle, a symphony movement by William Grant Still, a mariachi standard *son*, a Boulez orchestral work (derived from his own piano work), a hyperinstrument work by Tod Machover, a song cycle by Libby Larsen, and an orchestral work by Bright Sheng.
  - Complete multi-movement works for study (Baroque concerto and Classical symphony, concerto, chamber music, and sonata)
- Seven works by women composers, Middle Ages to contemporary (Hildegard von Bingen, Barbara Strozzi, Clara Schumann,

Fanny Mendelssohn Hensel, Amy Cheney Beach, Billie Holiday, Libby
Larsen)
- Numerous works influenced by traditional and world musics:
  - Traditional music of the Americas (Gottschalk piano work, Ives
    song, Copland ballet, Revueltas symphonic work, Bernstein musi-
    cal theater work, Cajun dance tune, mariachi *son*)
  - African influence (Still symphony, Ligeti piano etude, jazz selections)
  - European traditional music (Haydn string quartet, Gay ballad
    opera, Bizet opera, Ravel song cycle, Bartók orchestral work)
  - Middle and Far Eastern influence (Mozart sonata, Puccini opera,
    Mahler song cycle, Cage prepared piano work, Sheng orchestral work)

The appendices to *The Norton Scores* provide some useful pedagogical
resources for students and faculty. These include the following:

- a table of clefs and instrument transpositions;
- a table of instrument names and abbreviations in four languages
  (English, Italian, German, and French);
- a table of voice designations in English, Italian, and Latin;
- a table of scale degree names (in four languages);
- a glossary of all musical terms in the scores;
- a concordance among the scores, recordings, and listening guides
  in *The Enjoyment of Music*; and
- an index by genre and form of all selections in the anthology.

Volume I also has a helpful explanation of some performance practice issues
in early music, and, where needed, editor's notes explain particular markings
in a score that might not be widely understood.

There are many people to be thanked for their help in the preparation of
this Tenth Edition of *The Norton Scores*: my California State University, Long
Beach colleagues Roger Hickman, for his informative texts on each musical
selection and assistance with the selection of recorded performances, and
Gregory Maldonado, for his expert work on the highlighting of new scores;
my research assistants Denise Odello (University of California, Santa Barbara)
and Sarah Gerk (California State University, Long Beach) for their invaluable
help on this project; James Forney (St. Lawrence University) for his work
organizing the sound package; Tom Laskey of Sony Music, for his assistance
in the licensing and production of the recordings and their coordination with
the scores; Courtney Fitch and Graham Norwood, both of W. W. Norton, who
ably collected and edited the scores and handled the permissions; Kathy
Talalay of W. W. Norton, for her very skillful and painstaking work on the
entire *Enjoyment of Music* package; and Maribeth Payne, music editor at
W. W. Norton, for her support and guidance of this new edition. I am deeply
indebted to them all.

How to Follow the Highlighted Scores

By following the highlighted bands throughout a work, the listener will be able to read the score and recognize the most important or most audible musical lines. The following principles are illustrated on the facing page in an excerpt from Beethoven's Symphony No. 5 in C minor (first movement).

1. The musical line that is most prominent at any time is highlighted by a white band shown against light gray screening.
2. When a highlighted line continues from one system (group of staves) or page to the next, the white band ends with an arrow head (>) that indicates the continuation of the highlighted line, which begins on the next system with an indented arrow shape.
3. Multiple systems (more than one on a page) are separated by narrow white bands across the full width of the page. Watch carefully for these bands so that you do not overlook a portion of the score.
4. At times, two musical lines are highlighted simultaneously, indicating that they are equally audible. On first listening, it may be best to follow only one of these.
5. When more than one instrument plays the same musical line, in unison or octaves (this is called doubling), the instrument whose line is most audible is highlighted.
6. CD track numbers are given throughout the scores at the beginning of each movement and at important structural points within movements. They appear in a ☐ for the 8-CD set and in a ◇ for the 4-CD set, where appropriate.

A Note on the Recordings

Recordings of the works in *The Norton Scores* are available from the publisher. There is an 8-CD set that includes all the works in the two volumes of the anthology and a 4-CD set that includes selected works from both volumes. The recording track numbers are noted at the top of each score, to the right of the title.

Example (for Schubert's *Erlkönig*, in Volume 2)

8CD: 5/ 1 – 8
4CD: 2/ 57 – 64

The number after the colon gives the CD on which the work is included; the numbers in shapes are the inclusive track numbers of the work. For an overview of which works appear on the various recording sets, see Appendix D, *Concordance Table for Recordings*.

For the 8-CD package, the first set accompanies *The Norton Scores*, Volume 1, and the second set accompanies *The Norton Scores*, Volume 2.

Note: Occasionally, there are differences between the notated scores and the recordings; an editor's note is generally included in the score to explain these performance choices.

Electronic Listening Guides

There are interactive Listening Guides for each work in the Norton scores; these guides interact with the 8-CD and 4-CD sets, and the software is found on the Student Resource Disc (packaged with *The Enjoyment of Music*). These guides are a study tool to help students understand the form and style of each work.

A Note on the Performance Practice of Early Music

Performances of early music often vary somewhat from the printed score. These variants reflect changing interpretations of the performance practices of earlier eras. Also, because early notation was not as precise as that of modern times, certain decisions are left to the performer. Thus, there is no one "correct" way to perform a work.

1. Before around 1600, the decision to use voices or instruments and the choice of specific instruments were largely up to the performers. Thus, a vocal line may be played rather than sung, may alternate between voices and instruments, or may be sung with instruments doubling the part. In instrumental music, modern performances may vary widely in the instruments used.

2. In some of the earliest pieces, precise rhythmic interpretation is open to question; therefore, recordings will not always match the score. Bar lines, not used in early notation, have been added to most modern scores to facilitate metric interpretation.

3. In early notated music, the placement of words in relation to notes was rarely precise, leaving the text underlay to the performers. A modern edition presents one possible solution to the alignment of the words to the music, while a recording may present another possibility. Since languages were not standardized in early times, modern editions often maintain the text spellings of the original source, and performers sometimes follow historical rules of pronunciation.

4. Accidentals were added to medieval and Renaissance music by performers, according to certain rules. In modern scores, these accidentals (called *musica ficta*) are shown either above the notes or

on the staff in small type, as performance suggestions. Other editorial additions to scores are generally printed in italics (such as tempo markings and dynamics) or placed in square brackets.

5. In Baroque music, figured bass (consisting of a bass line and numbers indicating the harmonies to be played on a chordal instrument) was employed as a kind of shorthand from which musicians improvised, or "realized," the accompaniment at sight. In some modern scores, a suggested realization is provided by the editor, although performers may choose to play their own version of the accompaniment.

6. It was standard practice in music from the medieval era to the Classical period to improvise accompaniments and add embellishments to melodic lines, especially in repetitions of musical material. Today's performers often attempt to recreate this spontaneous style.

7. In earlier times, pitch varied according to the performance situation and the geographic locale. Modern replicas of historical instruments often sound at a lower pitch than today's standard (A = 440), and musicians occasionally choose to transpose music to a higher or lower key to facilitate performance.

I

Gregorian Chant

Kyrie (10th Century)

8CD: 1/ 1 – 3

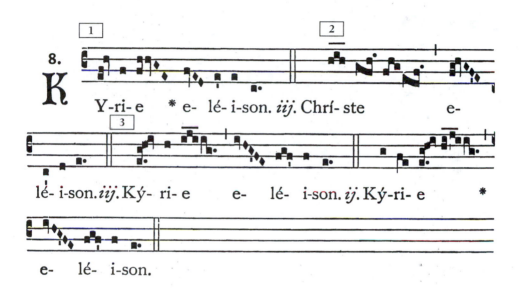

Editor's note: In this example from the *Liber usualis*, the number above the first initial indicates the chant is in mode 8, or hypomixolydian; the *iij* in the text is a repeat *(iterum)* sign, signifying that the text is sung three times; and the asterisk (*) signals a choral response.

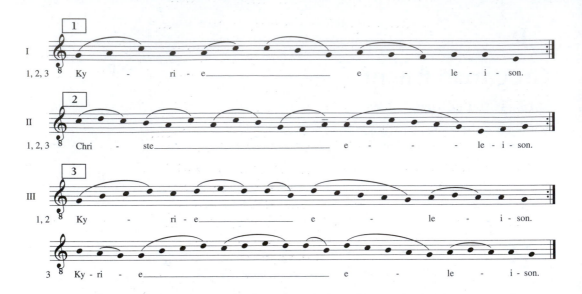

TEXT AND TRANSLATION

Kyrie eleison.	Lord, have mercy upon us.
Kyrie eleison.	Lord, have mercy upon us.
Kyrie eleison.	Lord, have mercy upon us.
Christe eleison.	Christ, have mercy upon us.
Christe eleison.	Christ, have mercy upon us.
Christe eleison.	Christ, have mercy upon us.
Kyrie eleison.	Lord, have mercy upon us.
Kyrie eleison.	Lord, have mercy upon us.
Kyrie eleison.	Lord, have mercy upon us.

The Kyrie is the first portion of the Mass service after the opening processional (Introit). The text consists of a threefold repetition of three acclamations: "Kyrie eleison," "Christe eleison," and "Kyrie eleison." These words are sung in every Mass service; the Kyrie, then, is the first section of the Mass Ordinary.

The musical setting maintains the tripartite division of the text: **A-A-A B-B-B C-C-C′**. Moving primarily with conjunct motion (stepwise), the entire melody lies within the range of an octave. Typical of tenth-century Kyries, each successive section increases in range, and the Christe and second Kyrie are both extended by melismas (singing of many notes to a single syllable). In keeping with standard performance practices, the chant is sung monophonically without a strict metric pulse. The alternation between a soloist and a choir, as heard in the recording, is called responsorial singing.

2

Hildegard von Bingen

Alleluia, O virga mediatrix
(*Alleluia, O mediating branch*) (mid-12th century)

8CD: 1/ 4 – 6
4CD: 1/ ◇1 – ◇3

al-le-lu — ia.*

O vir — ga, me-di-a-trix,

sancta vi-sce-ra tu – a mor —

tem su-per-a-ve-runt, et ven-

Editor's note: In the transcription that follows, slurs show compound neumes (or signs denoting multiple notes); small notes show a particular kind of single neume (diamond-shaped in the original notation), and slashed eighth notes show a passing note that should be only half-vocalized, or sung lightly. Because there are differing manuscript sources for this chant, the recording varies slightly from the original notation shown here and the transcription.

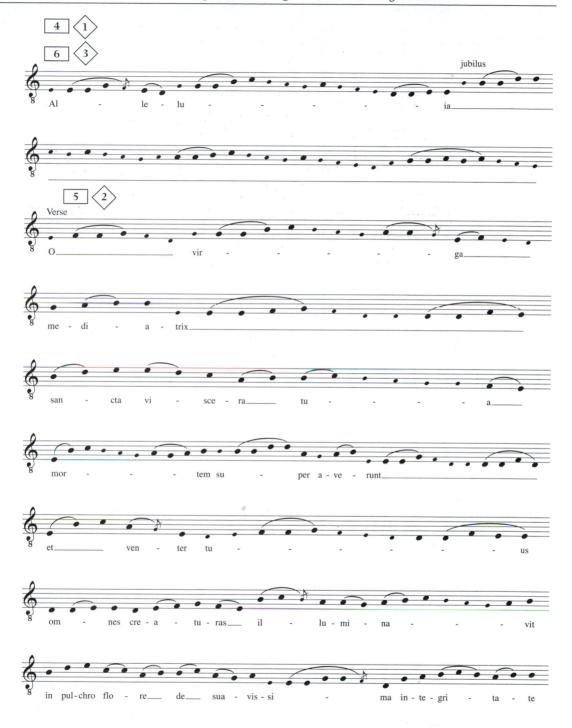

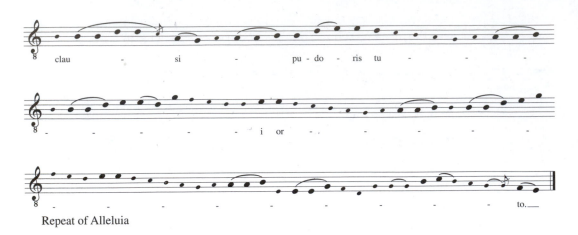

clau - si - pu - do - ris tu - - -

- i or - , - - -

- - - - - - to.___

Repeat of Alleluia

TEXT AND TRANSLATION

Alleluia.	Alleluia.
O virga mediatrix	O mediating branch
sancta viscera tua mortem superaverunt,	Your holy flesh has overcome death,
et venter tuus omnes creaturas illuminavit	And your womb has illuminated all creatures
in pulchro flore de suavissima integritate	Through the beautiful flower of your tender purity
clausi pudoris tui orto.	That sprang from your chastity.
Alleluia.	Alleluia.

Hildegard von Bingen (1098–1179) is one of the most fascinating figures of the Middle Ages. A visionist, composer, and writer of science, philosophy, poetry, and drama, she founded her own convent in Rupertsberg, Germany, and served as abbess there. Her twelfth-century Alleluia provides a beautiful example of the late medieval style and of Hildegard's remarkable talents as a poet and composer.

The Alleluia follows the Gradual in the Mass service and is part of the musical response to the Scripture lessons. The text can be seen in an **A-B-A** pattern; the **A** portions contain the single word "Alleluia," and the **B** presents a Verse that is appropriate to the particular feast day. Since this text changes for every service, the chant is part of the Mass Proper.

Musical settings of Alleluias generally retain the **A-B-A** structure of the text and follow a traditional pattern of responsorial singing (alternating soloist and choir). The Alleluia begins with an intonation by a soloist. The chorus then repeats the opening phrase and continues with a lengthy melisma on the last syllable (-*ia*), called a *jubilus*. The Verse is sung either by a soloist with a brief choral response or by the soloist without a response, as in this example. At the return of the Alleluia, the chorus repeats the opening phrase and the *jubilus*.

Hildegard's Verse, which reflects the late medieval fascination with the Virgin Mary, pays homage and joyful reverence to Christ's Mother. The initial section is primarily set in a neumatic manner and does not venture far from the *finalis* (final tone). But with the references to "womb," "flower," and "chasity," Hildegard supports these images with extended melismas, an expanded range, and her signature leaps of a fifth. The melody dramatically climaxes on a G, which is heard twice at the parallel melismas for "tui" and "orto." Hildegard gives the entire work a sense of unity by making several melodic references to the Alleluia, most notably at the beginning and end of the Verse. Since Hildegard's chants were likely sung at her convent, performances by woman were considered acceptable in her day, as they are today.

3

Notre Dame School

Organum, *Gaude Maria virgo* (*Rejoice Mary, virgin*), excerpt
(early 13th century)

8CD: 1/ 7 – 8
4CD: 1/ 4 – 5

Triplum

Duplum

Tenor

*Norton recording fades out here.

TEXT AND TRANSLATION

Gaude Maria	Rejoice Mary
virgo cunctas hereses sola	O virgin, you alone have
interemisti.	destroyed all heresies.

The earliest examples of polyphony, called *organum*, appear in the Gradual and Alleluia from the Mass and the Responsory from the Offices. All three chants are responsorial, both in their function as a musical response to Scripture readings and in their performance practice of alternating solo and choral sections (the choir literally responds to a soloist). Polyphony appears only during the solo passages of these chants.

A significant repertory of such works was created at the Notre Dame Cathedral in Paris during the twelfth and thirteenth centuries. Distinctive of Notre Dame polyphony is the addition of between one and three quickly moving melodic lines over the long, sustained notes of the original chant. The Responsory *Gaude Maria virgo (Rejoice Mary, virgin)* is sung at Vespers and Matins for the Purification of the Virgin (February 2) and at Matins for the Feast of Circumcision (January 1). In this excerpt, the opening solo intonation is set in polyphony, while the chorus portion, beginning with the word "virgo," is sung in monophonic chant. In the solo section, the original chant is in the bottom voice (Tenor), and the newly composed upper voices (Duplum and Triplum) sing an extended melisma with a strong rhythmic pulse. This three-part polyphonic texture is typical of the thirteenth-century style of Pérotin. Based on the repetitive pattern of a rhythmic mode, the upper voices primarily alternate between long and short notes. The Duplum and the Triplum have similar ranges and frequently interchange material.

4

Anonymous

Motet, *Mout me fu grief/ Robin m'aime/ Portare* (*Greatly grieved am I/ Robin loves me/ To carry*) (13th Century)

9   Instrumental performance

10   Vocal performance

Mout me fu grief li de - par - tir de m'a - mi - e - te, la jo - lie au cler vis,

Ro - bin m'ai - me, Ro - bin m'a; Ro - bin m'a

Portare

qui est blanche et ver - mel - le - te com - me ro - se par de - sus lis, ce m'est a -

de - man - de - e, si m'a - vra. Ro - bin m'a cha -

vis; son tres douz ris mi fait fre - mir et si oell vair ri - ant lan -

ta cor - roi - e et au - mon - nie - re de soi - e,

TEXT AND TRANSLATION

Top voice:

Mout me fu grief li departir de m'amiete,	The departure of my dear sweetheart grieved me deeply,
la jolie au cler vis,	the pretty one with the bright face,
qui est blanche et vermellete comme rose par desus lis,	as white and vermillion as rose set against lily
ce m'est avis;	or so it seems to me;
son tres douz ris mi fait fremir et si oell vair riant languir.	her ever so sweet laughter makes me tremble, and her gray-blue eyes, languish.
Ha Dieus, com mar la lessai!	O God, woe that I left her!
Blanchete comme flour de lis	Little white lily flower,
quant vous verrai?	when will I see you?

Dame de valour,	Worthy Lady,
vermelle comme rose en mai,	red as a rose in May,
pour vous sui en grant dolour.	on your account I suffer great grief.

Middle voice:

Robin m'aime, Robin m'a;	Robin loves me, Robin has me;
Robin m'a demandee, si m'avra.	Robin asked for me, and he will have me.
Robin m'achata corroie	Robin bought me a belt
Et aumonniere de soie;	and a little purse of silk;
Pour quoi done ne l'ameroie?	Why then would I not love him?
Aleuriva!	Aleuriva!
Robin m'aime, Robin m'a;	Robin loves me, Robin has me;
Robin m'a demandee, si m'avra.	Robin asked for me, and he will have me.

Tenor (bottom voice):

Portare

Mout me fu grief/Robin m'aime/Portare exhibits the standard three-voice texture of the thirteenth-century motet. The work is polytextual (each voice has its own text), featuring both French and Latin and mixing secular and sacred subjects. Typical of the genre at this time, the bottom voice derives its pitches from a Gregorian chant. The text of the upper voice uses descriptive words associated with the Virgin Mary ("white lily flower" and "worthy lady"), and hence can be linked to the sacred tenor line. By contrast, the middle voice describes the much earthier relationship between Robin and Marion, the famed lovers of the Robin Hood legend.

Unusual for motets of this time is the borrowing not only of phrases of other melodies in the top voice but also of a complete trouvère song in the middle voice. The song, attributed to Adam de la Halle, is presented in its original rondeau structure: **A-B-a-a-b-A-B** (capital letters refer to repeated texts). In terms of modern notation, the **A** phrases are two measures in length, and the **B** phrases have three measures. This repetitive structure is mirrored in the tenor, with some slight variations. The upper voice, the most rhythmically active line, remains independent from these repetitions. The frequent cadence points are supported with perfect fifths or unisons.

Although written for voices, motets could be performed instrumentally or with voices and instruments combined. In the recording accompanying this anthology, the motet can be heard twice. The first time, on instruments alone, features an organ on the top voice, a bowed fiddle (predecessor to the violin) on the middle voice, and a lute on the bottom. In the repeat of the motet, a soprano and tenor sing the top two lines, doubled by the instruments. Perhaps typical of the era, the tenor line remains instrumental throughout.

5

Raimbaut de Vaquieras

Troubador dance song, *Kalenda maya* (*The First of May*)
(late 12th century)

1. vos, do- na ve-   ra- ia,   e cha- ia de pla- ia .lge- los, anz qe.m
2. ja mais no.m vei- ri- a;   cell di- a mor- ri- a don- na pros, q'ie.us
3. ai, ni d'als ven- cu- da;   vol gu- da, cre- su- da vos ai ses autr'
4. danz qi.ils vos gra- zi- ra,   qe.us mi- ra, cos- si- ra cui- danz, don cors
5. vetz e co- neis-   sen- sa;   va- len- sa ses ten- sa vi- tetz ab ben-
6. ses q'E- recs E-   ni- da.   Ba- sti- da, fi- ni- da, n'En gles, ai l'e-

1. n'e- stra-   ia   e ja- ia e.m tra- ia vas vos do- na ve-   ra-
2. per- dri-   a.
3. a-   ju-   da.
4. se- spi-   ra.
5. vo- len-   sa.
6. stam-pi-   da.

ia,   e cha- ia de pla- ia .l ge- los, anz qe.m n'e- stra-   ia.

TRANSLATION

11 ⟨**6**⟩ Instrumental Performance

12 ⟨**7**⟩ Strophe 1 — Neither May Day nor the beech tree's leaves nor the song of birds nor gladiolus flowers are pleasing to me, noble and vivacious lady, until I receive a swift messenger from your fair person to tell me of some new pleasure that love brings me; and may I be joined to you and drawn toward you, perfect lady; and may the jealous one fall stricken before I must leave you.

13 ⟨**8**⟩ Strophe 2 — My sweet beloved, for the sake of God, may the jealous one never laugh at my pain, for his jealousy would be very costly if it were to separate two such lovers; for I would never be joyful again, nor would joy be of any benefit to me without you; I would set out on such a road that no one would ever see me again; on that day would I die, worthy lady, that I lost you.

14 ⟨**9**⟩ Strophe 3 — How shall my lady be lost, or restored to me, if she has not yet been mine? For a man or woman is not a lover just by thinking so. But when a suitor is accepted as a lover, the reputation that he gains is greatly enhanced, and the attractive appearance causes much stir; but I have not held you naked nor conquered you in any other sense, I have only desired you and believed in you, without any further encouragement.

Strophe 4 (not on recording)

I should not likely find pleasure if I should ever be separated from you, Fair Knight, in anger; for my being is not turned toward anyone else, my desire does not draw me to anyone else, for I desire none but you. I know that this would be pleasing to slanderers, my lady, since this is the only thing that would satisfy them. There are those who would be grateful to you if they were to see or feel my suffering, since they admire you and think presumptuously about that which makes the heart sigh.

Strophe 5 (not on recording)

Lady Beatrice, your worth is so refined by its nature, and it develops and grows beyond that of all other ladies; in my opinion you enhance your dominance with your merit and your admirable speech without fail; you are responsible for initiating praiseworthy actions; you have wisdom patience and learning; incontestably, you adorn your worth with benevolence.

15 ⟨10⟩ Strophe 6

Worthy lady, everyone praises and proclaims your merit which is so pleasing; and whoever would forget you places little value on his life; therefore I worship you, distinguished lady, for I have singled you out as the most pleasing and the best accomplished in worth, and I have courted you and served you better then Eric did Enide. Lord Engles,* I have constructed and completed the estampida.

Troubadour songs are among the earliest surviving examples of secular music. One of the most colorful figures in this tradition is Raimbaut de Vaqueiras (c. 1155–1207), who began his career as a *jongleur* (performer) and was elevated to a knightly status after saving the life of one of his patrons in battle. According to his *vida* (biography), Raimbaut improvised the words to *Kalenda maya* on hearing the tune played by two jongleurs as an *estampie,* an

*Boniface, Marquis of Monferrat, patron.

early medieval dance. Indeed, the tune takes the shape of a standard estampie with three repeated phrases: **A-A-B-B-C-C**. Typical of this dance form, the **B** phrases alternate open and closed cadences.

The overall form of the song is strophic; the same tune is repeated for each of the poetic stanzas. While celebrating the coming of spring, the poet pledges to continue to love and admire his lady from afar, although he seems to delight in making her husband jealous. Using a dialect known as *langue d'oc*, Raimbaut cleverly plays with a repetitive rhyme scheme. In the first stanza, the primary rhyme is established with the word "maya." In the two **A** phrases, this sound occurs six times, each time set with a descending melodic motion of two or three notes. Similarly, the **B** phrases conclude with the same rhyme and three-note cadences. The **C** phrases begin with two quick references to the rhyme, both with descending gestures, and end with a final rhyme and descent. The word "d'auzell" provides an internal rhyme, usually appearing in less prominent positions. The same poetic formula is used for each stanza.

Since the melody lies within the range of an octave and moves predominantly in conjunct motion, the tune could be sung or played by a variety of medieval instruments. In the recording that accompanies this anthology, a *rebec* (a three-string predecessor of the violin), a pipe (a three-holed, end-blown flute), a *guitarra moresca* (a strummed string instrument introduced into Spain by the Moors), and *nakers* (small hand drums) can be heard. Also subject to a variety of interpretations for this song are the rhythmic values and accidentals, as evidenced in the several discrepancies between the score and the recording.

6

Guillaume de Machaut

Rondeau, *Puis qu'en oubli* (*Since I am forgotten*)
(mid-14th century)

8CD: 1/ 16 – 20
4CD: 1/ ⟨11⟩ – ⟨15⟩

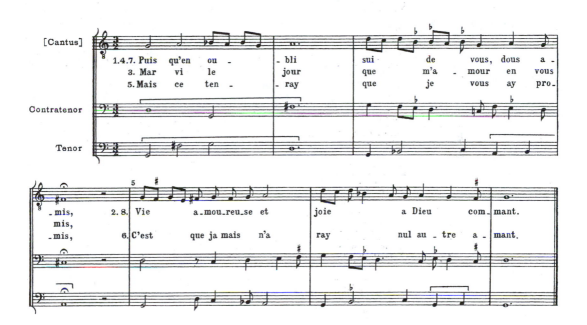

Editor's note: The numbers next to the text signal the order in which to perform the two sections of the rondeau. The bracketed notes were originally written as ligatures—notational devices that combined two or more notes into a single symbol. CD track numbers are given on p. 18 next to the text and translation.

TEXT AND TRANSLATION

16	⟨11⟩	Refrain	Puis qu'en oubli sui de vous, dous amis, Vie amoureuse et joie a Dieu commant.	Since I am forgotten by you, sweet friend, I bid farewell to a life of love and joy.
17	⟨12⟩	Verse	Mar vi le jour que m'amour en vous mis;	Unlucky was the day I placed my love in you;
18	⟨13⟩	Partial refrain	Puis qu'en oubli sui de vous, dous amis.	Since I am forgotten by you, sweet friend.
19	⟨14⟩	Verse	Mais ce tenray que je vous ay promis: C'est que jamais n'aray nul autre amant.	But what was promised you I will sustain: That I shall never have any other love.
20	⟨15⟩	Refrain	Puis qu'en oubli sui de vous, dous amis, Vie amoureuse et joie a Dieu commant.	Since I am forgotten by you, sweet friend, I bid farewell to a life of love and joy.

Guillaume de Machaut, (c. 1300–1377), who achieved greatness in both poetry and music, can be seen as a late-medieval counterpart to the troubadours and trouvères. At the same time, his polyphonic secular music looks forward to the chanson of the early Renaissance. Machaut was a key figure in establishing the fixed poetic forms that would dominate secular music for over a century. The rondeau *Puis qu'en oubli (Since I am forgotten)* exhibits the standard **A-B-a-A-a-b-A-B** structure associated with the poetic genre. The subject is a traditional theme of courtly love—unrequited and unhappy love. But Machaut's reiterated refrains of "Since I am forgotten by you, sweet friend" and "I bid farewell to a life of love and joy" create an added poignancy and sense of pain.

Also indicative of future developments is the three-part texture. The setting with the principal melody in the top line accompanied by two lower lines will remain in vogue in secular music until the time of Josquin. The low range of the principal melodic line suggests a performance either by three men or by a solo male voice with instrumental accompaniment. The angular melodies and the prominent double-leading-tone cadence at the end of the **B** section are distinctive of the fourteenth century.

7

Guillaume Du Fay

L'homme armé Mass (*The Armed Man* Mass),
Kyrie (1460s)

21   *L'homme armé* (Anonymous tune)

TEXT AND TRANSLATION

L'homme, l'homme, l'homme armé,
L'homme armé doibt on doubter.

On a fait partout crier

Que chascun se viengue armer

D'un haubregon de fer.

L'homme, l'homme, l'homme armé
L'homme, armé doibt on doubter.

The armed man,
The armed man is to be
   feared.

The cry has been raised all
   around,

that everyone must arm
   himself

with an iron hauberk [coat
   of mail].

The armed man,
The armed man is to be
   feared.

Kyrie

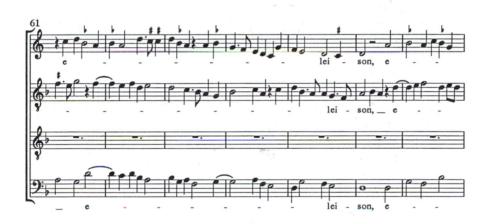

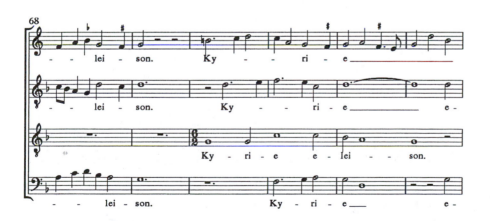

TEXT AND TRANSLATION

Kyrie I

Kyrie, eleison.	Lord, have mercy upon us.
Kyrie, eleison.	Lord, have mercy upon us.
Kyrie, eleison.	Lord, have mercy upon us.

Christe

Christe, eleison.	Christ, have mercy upon us.
Christe, eleison.	Christ, have mercy upon us.
Christe, eleison.	Christ, have mercy upon us.

Kyrie II

Kyrie, eleison.	Lord, have mercy upon us.
Kyrie, eleison.	Lord, have mercy upon us.
Kyrie, eleison.	Lord, have mercy upon us.

In the early Renaissance, composers began setting the five principal sections of the Mass Ordinary as a cycle, unified by a common melody called a *cantus firmus* (literally "fixed melody") in the Tenor of each section. Du Fay (c. 1397–1474) was one of the first composers to use the secular tune *L'homme armé* (*The Armed Man*) as a cantus firmus for a cyclic Mass. The tune, set with long rhythmic values, appears in the Tenor line throughout the Mass and provides a structural framework for each movement. In the Kyrie, the tune's tripartite form (**A-B-A**) coincides with the three sections of the Kyrie, with slight modifications. In each of the three sections, the entrance of the Tenor is delayed, creating a reduced voicing that expands with the entrance of the cantus firmus. The duetting nature of the upper voices is most prominent at the opening of the Christe.

Other early Renaissance features can be observed. The *a cappella* setting for four voices, the triadic passing harmonies, and the emphasis on counterpoint (primarily nonimitative) reflect the new style of the fifteenth century. Ties to the medieval past can be seen in the perfect harmonies at major cadences, the similarity of the four vocal ranges (all sung by men), and the melodic dominance of the upper voices.

8

Josquin des Prez

Motet, *Ave Maria . . . virgo serena* (*Hail Mary . . . gentle virgin*) (*1480s?*)

8CD: 1/ 25 – 31
4CD: 1/ ⟨16⟩ – ⟨22⟩

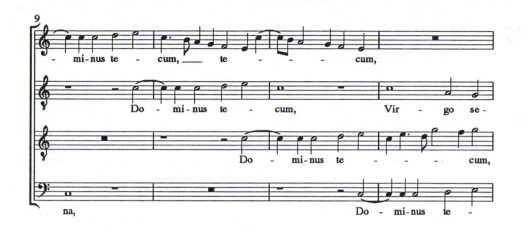

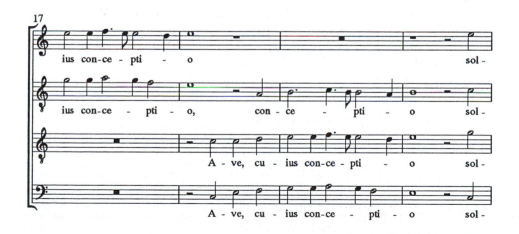

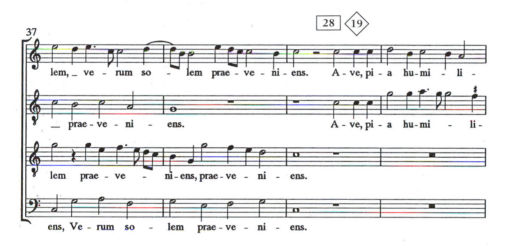

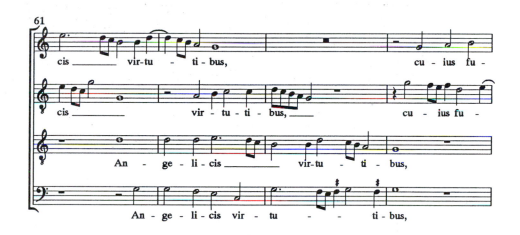

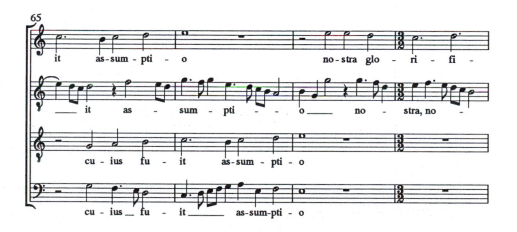

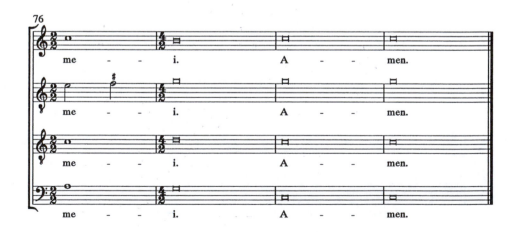

TEXT AND TRANSLATION

Ave Maria, gratia plena,	Hail Mary, full of grace,
Dominus tecum, virgo serena.	The Lord is with you, gentle Virgin.
Ave cujus conceptio	Hail, whose conception,
Solemni plena gaudio	Full of solemn joy,
Caelestia, terrestria,	Fills the heaven, the earth,
Nova replet laetitia.	With new rejoicing.
Ave cujus nativitas	Hail, whose birth
Nostra fuit solemnitas,	Was our festival,
Ut lucifer lux oriens,	As our luminous rising light
Verum solem praeveniens.	Coming before the true sun.
Ave pia humilitas,	Hail, pious humility,
Sine viro fecunditas,	Fertility without a man,
Cujus annuntiatio,	Whose annunciation
Nostra fuit salvatio.	Was our salvation.
Ave vera virginitas,	Hail, true virginity,
Immaculata castitas,	Unspotted chastity,
Cujus purificatio	Whose purification
Nostra fuit purgatio.	Was our cleansing.
Ave praeclara omnibus	Hail, famous with all
Angelicis virtutibus,	Angelic virtues,
Cujus fuit assumptio	Whose assumption was
Nostra glorificatio.	Our glorification.
O Mater Dei,	O Mother of God,
Memento mei.	Remember me.
Amen.	Amen.

The Renaissance motet, unlike its medieval counterpart, is a setting of a single text on a sacred subject in Latin. In its broadest definition, the term can be applied to any polyphonic composition based on a Catholic Latin text other than the Ordinary of the Mass. The text of the motet *Ave Maria . . . virgo serena* (*Hail Mary . . . gentle virgin*) by Josquin des Prez (c. 1450–1521) is a Latin poem praising the Virgin Mary. Consisting of an opening couplet, five quatrains, and a closing couplet, the poem contains a simple rhyme scheme. The acclamation "Ave" is the initial word for the opening couplet and for all five quatrains.

The repetitive structure of the poem is reflected in the music, but Josquin masterfully creates a continuous, nearly seamless flow. Although this motet is intended for male voices (ideally *a cappella*), the vocal ranges are more distinct than those in Du Fay's Mass. The bass voice has been extended lower, and the top voice would have been sung by boy sopranos. Josquin creates variety by alternating chordal and imitative textures and by changing the number and combination of voices. The texture is frequently divided between the two upper voices and the two lower voices, and these pairs alternate in imitative fashion. The fourth quatrain (beginning in m. 47) is set in a chordal texture, yet contains a canon separated by one beat between the soprano and tenor. Indicative of the early date for this work (probably from the 1480s), the major cadences still close with open-fifth harmonies.

9

Giovanni Pierluigi da Palestrina

Pope Marcellus Mass, Gloria (published 1567)

8CD: 1/ 32 – 33
4CD: 1/ ⟨23⟩ – ⟨24⟩

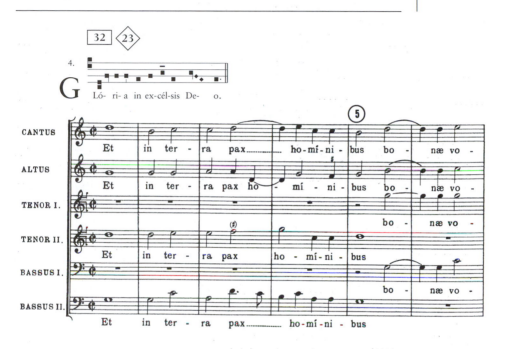

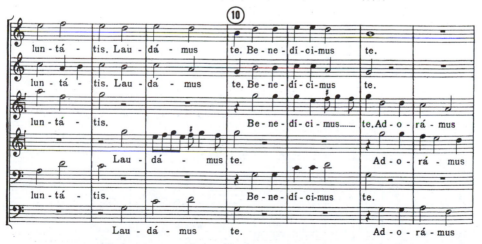

TEXT AND TRANSLATION

Gloria in excelsis Deo	Glory be to God on high,
et in terra pax hominibus	and on earth peace to men
bonae voluntatis.	of good will.
Laudamus te.	We praise Thee.
Benedicimus te.	We bless Thee.
Adoramus te.	We adore Thee.
Glorificamus te.	We glorify Thee.
Gratias agimus tibi propter	We give Thee thanks for
magnam gloriam tuam.	Thy great glory.
Domine Deus, Rex caelestis,	Lord God, heavenly King,
Deus Pater omnipotens.	God the Father Almighty.
Domine Fili	O Lord, the only-begotten Son,

unigenite, Jesu Christe.	Jesus Christ.
Domine Deus, Agnus Dei,	Lord God, Lamb of God,
Filius Patris.	Son of the Father.
Qui tollis	Thou that takest away
peccata mundi,	the sins of the world,
miserere nobis.	Have mercy on us.
Qui tollis peccata mundi,	Thou that takest away the sins
suscipe deprecationem nostram.	Of the world, receive our prayer.
Qui sedes ad dexteram Patris,	Thou that sittest at the right hand
miserere nobis.	of the Father, have mercy on us.
Quoniam tu solus sanctus.	For thou alone art holy.
Tu solus Dominus.	Thou only art the Lord.
Tu solus Altissimus.	Thou alone art most high.
Jesu Christe, cum Sancto Spiritu	Jesus Christ, along with the Holy Spirit
in gloria Dei Patris.	in the glory of God the Father.
Amen.	Amen.

Giovanni Pierluigi da Palestrina (c. 1525–1594), a composer of over one hundred Masses, can be seen as the foremost musical representative of the Counter-Reformation movement in Rome. Responding to the challenge of the Reformation, the Council of Trent suggested reforms for the Catholic Church, even focusing attention on music. In particular, concerns were expressed about words being obscured by careless pronunciation and complicated counterpoint. According to a popular anecdote, the Council considered completely banning polyphony from services, but was convinced by the beauty and clarity of Palestrina's *Pope Marcellus* Mass (1567) to refrain from such action.

Although the validity of the story is questionable, the resulting reputation has made this Mass one of the most celebrated sacred works of the era. The declamation of the text in the Gloria, primarily set in a six-part homophonic texture, certainly adheres to the guidelines of the Council. Variety is created through changes in register and in the number of voices singing at any given moment. The final "Amen" section contains the only suggestion of the pervasive imitative style that characterizes late Renaissance sacred music.

IO

Giovanni Gabrieli

Motet, *O quam suavis* (*O how sweet*) (published 1615)

8CD: 1/ 34 – 35

TEXT AND TRANSLATION

O quam suavis est, Domine,   O how sweet, Lord, is your spirit,
   spiritus tuus;
qui, ut dulcedinem tuam   who demonstrates your sweetness
in filios demonstrares,   to your sons
pane suavissimo de caelo praestito,   by providing the sweetest bread from
                                          heaven;
esurientes reples bonis,   you fill the hungry with good things,
fastidiosos divites dimittens inanes.   and send the rich and scornful away
                                          empty.

The transition from the Renaissance to the Baroque can most dramatically be seen in the polychoral motets of Giovanni Gabrieli. (c. 1557–1612). While retaining some ties to the Renaissance style, Gabrieli moves away from the *a cappella* sound and pervasive imitation of the previous generation and exploits the potency of a newer, more homorhythmic musical style. *O quam suavis* (*O how sweet*), a setting of a text from the Vespers service for the Feast of Corpus Christi, was published posthumously in Gabrieli's second book of *Sacrae Symphoniae* (*Sacred Symphonies,* 1615). Reflecting the polychoral tradition associated with the St. Mark's Cathedral in Venice, the motet is divided into two choirs. Both contain four voices; the first choir is set for cantus (highest part), alto, tenor, and bass, and the second is set for a lower ensemble of alto, two tenors, and a bass. In keeping with appropriate performance practices, the recorded performance uses boy sopranos and sackbuts (similar to the modern trombones), which double a number of the lower vocal lines.

The change in musical conception can be seen in the more declamatory melodic style that sometimes creates a sense of dialogue between the two choirs. At times, the quick melodic turns and dotted rhythms suggest an instrumental, rather than vocal, conception. The strong emotional quality created by these brief motives, the antiphonal singing of the two choirs, and the chromatic harmonies point to the emerging Baroque style. Also indicative of the newer style are the mixture of voices and instruments and the presence of an organ basso continuo.

II

Josquin des Prez

Chanson, *Mille regretz* (*A thousand regrets*)
(1520)

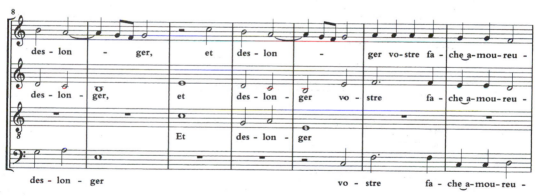

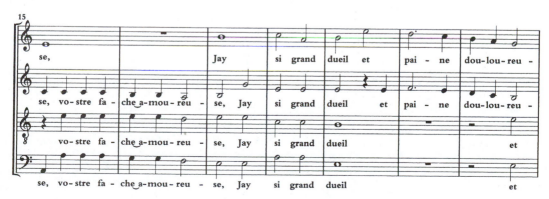

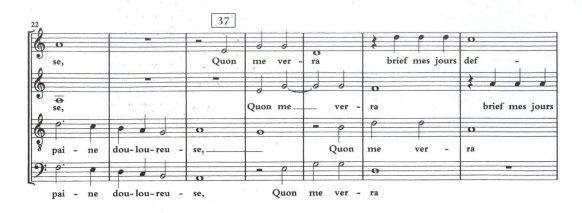

TEXT AND TRANSLATION

Mille regretz de vous habandonner
Et d'eslonger vostre fache amoureuse,
Jay si grand dueil et paine douloureuse,
Qu'on me verra brief mes jours definer.

A thousand regrets for deserting you
And leaving behind your loving face,
I have such great sorrow and grievous pain,
That one can see that my days will not be long.

Mille regretz (*A thousand regrets*), which may have been written for Charles V in 1520, exemplifies the Renaissance conception of the secular song. Abandoning the fixed poetic forms of the late Middle Ages, Josquin sets a simple four-line love poem. The treble-dominated three-part texture characteristic of earlier secular songs gives way to an expressive four-part setting. Since the work is secular, performances could have involved female singers and instrumentalists. In this recording, the *a cappella* ideal is retained.

Although much of *Mille regretz* displays a homorhythmic texture, each voice plays an independent role in the work as a whole. The chanson presents several points of imitation, either involving all four voices (mm. 24–27) or pairs of voices (mm. 19–24). The use of overlapping cadences allows the music to flow without breaks until the closing section (m. 34), which echoes the final phrase of the poem three times. Josquin creates a pervading sense of sadness in this work through the continuously descending melodic phrases and the choice of Phrygian mode.

12

Tielman Susato

Three Dances (published 1551)

8CD: 1/ 38 – 41
4CD: 1/ ⟨25⟩ – ⟨28⟩

Ronde I

41 ⟨28⟩ (after Ronde III)

Editor's note: Ornamentation and musica ficta (implied accidentals added editorially above the notes) heard on the Norton recording are the interpretation of the performers. This set closes with a return to the second section of this dance, followed by an added bow chord.

Ronde 2

Ronde 3

*The recording omits the last four measures the first time through this section. A four-measure transition to Ronde 3 is added by the performers, based on the opening phrase of Ronde 1, to modulate to the new key.

Returns to Ronde 1, last section, played twice.

Tielman Susato (c. 1515–c. 1571), a prominent music publisher in Antwerp, issued a collection of dances entitled *Danserye*. Many of the works are arrangements of well known chansons. Indeed, Ronde 2 of this anthology is drawn from a bawdy song by a French composer. Susato, himself a professional sackbut player, arranged these works for amateur performers. His dedication to the book reads:

> Music is . . .
>
> a unique heavenly gift to humanity,
>
> intended to praise God with thanks,
>
> to dispel idleness, to pass the time,
>
> to chase away melancholy,
>
> to ease heavy minds,
>
> and to gladden
>
> worried hearts.

Included in this 1551 publication is a set of three rondes, each of which is in a quick duple meter. Originally a country dance, the *ronde* became fashionable with city folk and aristocrats in the mid-sixteenth century. Each ronde is binary (**A-A-B-B**), a typical dance form for the late Renaissance and Baroque. After the three dances have been played, the second section of the first dance is repeated, rounding off the set as a whole.

The four-part texture of each dance moves primarily in homorhymic motion, and the melody unfolds in four- or eight-measure phrases. For the most part, each line lies within an octave and could be played by a variety of Renaissance instruments. In the recording, the dances feature double-reed instruments (shawms), brass (sackbut and cornet), and percussion.

13

Claudio Monteverdi

Madrigal, *Ecco mormorar l'onde*
(*Here, now, the waves murmur*) (1590)

8CD: 1/ 42 – 44
4CD: 1/ 29 – 31

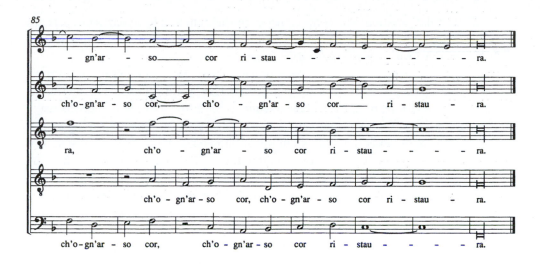

TEXT AND TRANSLATION

Ecco mormorar l'onde	Here, now, the wave murmur
e tremolar le fronde	And the leaves and young poplars tremble
a l'aura matutina e gli arborscelli,	In the morning breeze
[Ecco mormorar . . .]	[Here, now, the waves murmur . . .]
e sovria i verdi rami i vaghi augelli	And upon the green branches the enchanting birds
contra soavemente,	Sing sweetly,
e rider l'oriente.	And the East smiles.
Ecco già l'alba appare	Here, now, the dawn breaks
e si specchia nel mare,	And is mirrored in the sea,
e rasserena il cielo,	And calms the sky,
e imperla il dolce gielo,	And adorns the light frost with pearls,
e gli alti monti indora.	And gilds the towering mountains.
Oh, bella e vag'aurora,	O lovely, gentle dawn,
l'aura è tua messaggiera, e tu de l'aura	The breeze is your messenger, and you of the breeze
ch'ogni arso cor ristaura!	That restores every heavy heart.

Monteverdi's five-voice *Ecco mormorar l'onde*, published in his *Second Book of Madrigals* (1590), reflects several characteristics of the Italian madrigal of the late sixteenth century. The through-composed structure features imitative counterpoint with occasional homorhythmic passages that mark significant cadences. The setting of each line reflects Monteverdi's evident concern with text declamation. The contrast between the high and low voices was perhaps inspired by the new virtuosic vocal style of the professional women singers from Ferrara—the *Concerto delle donne*.

The variety of nature images provided by Torquato Tasso's poem is vividly reflected in Monteverdi's word painting. The opening line, "Ecco mormorar l'onde" (Here, now, the waves murmur) is set in the tenor with a gentle rising and falling motion, suggesting a wave. The idea is imitated in the basso and alto voices, and even reflected in the quinto and canto parts. Two new images are quickly introduced: an undulating motive for "e tremolar le fronde" (and the leaves and young poplars tremble), and an extended melisma for "a l'aura matutina e gli arborscelli" (in the morning breeze). These motives are playfully interchanged before the madrigal comes to its first major cadence at measure 26. Other images follow, including another lively melisma for the birds that "cantar soavemente" (sing sweetly) and a strong rising line for "gli alti monti" (the towering mountains). The final line, "ch'ogni arso cor ristaura!" (that restores every heavy heart), projects a contrasting mood that brings the madrigal to a more somber close.

14

John Farmer

Madrigal, *Fair Phyllis* (published 1599)

8CD: 1/ 45 – 46
4CD: 1/ 32 – 33

Following the appearance of *Musica Transalpina* in 1588, madrigals became all the rage in England. The English madrigal differs from its Italian model in its generally lighter tone. Despite the presence of great English poets at the time, including Shakespeare, the choice of poetry does not match the high quality often found in Italian settings. Moreover, the texture tends to be more melodically oriented, with the principal musical interest lying in the top voice.

Fair Phyllis appears in John Farmer's only publication of four-part madrigals (1599). Following the tradition of the lighter madrigal style established by Thomas Morley, Farmer sets this idyllic poetic vision with contrasting homorhythmic and polyphonic sections. He creates a playful mood through word painting and subtle metric shifts, such as the delightful triple meter at the end. In the tradition of the Italian madrigal, the final line of text is repeated, which Farmer (fl. 1591–1601) uses to underscore the humor of his amorous word painting.

15

Claudio Monteverdi

L'incoronazione di Poppea (*The Coronation of Poppea*),
Act III, Scene 7 (1642)

8CD: 1/ 47 – 51

Editor's note: In the Norton recording, the consuls and tribunes are sung as solos.
Throughout the score, footnotes refer to two manuscript sources, one in Naples (N),
and the other in Venice (V).

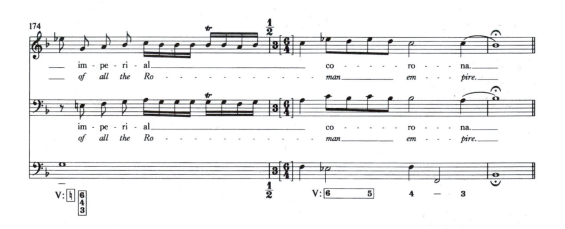

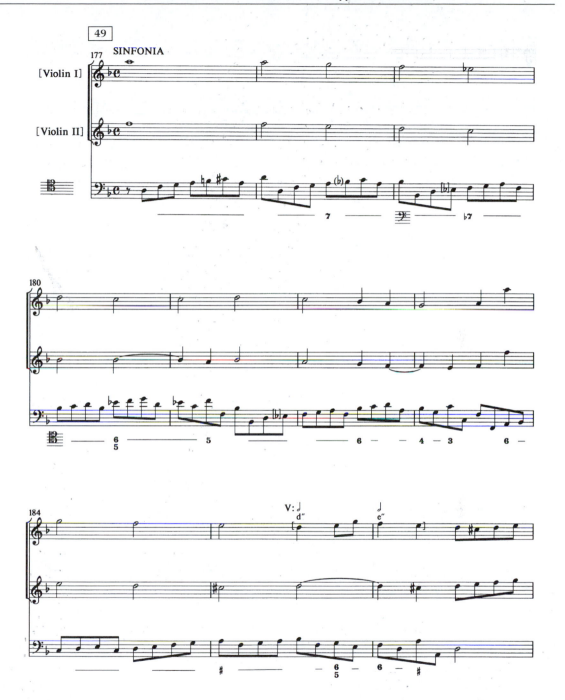

Editor's note: Norton recording omits the Ritornello (measures 339–343), but adds an instrumental introduction based on the ground-bass figure. The role of Nero, originally a castrato, is sung on the Norton recording by a mezzo-soprano.

Composed in the year prior to the composer's death, Monteverdi's *The Coronation of Poppea* (1642) stands as a masterpiece of early Baroque opera. The original final scene has been lost, and the version that comes down to us today is the product of revisions made by younger contemporaries. The libretto created by Giovanni Busenello deals with a historical episode in the unsavory life of the Roman emperor Nero. Seduced by the beauty and charms of the courtesan Poppea, Nero divorces his wife (and has her executed) in order to remarry. His principal adviser, the philosopher Seneca, is also condemned to death for his opposition to Nero's decision. The final coronation scene for Poppea may seem like the triumph of evil over good, but Monteverdi's audience would likely have known that Poppea was killed within three years, reportedly kicked to death in a fit of anger by Nero.

The coronation scene comprises two principal vocal sections. The first, an intricate duet in which the consuls pay tribute to the new queen, contains both a recitative and an aria-like passage in triple meter. The elaborate cadential motion includes an example of *stile concitato* (agitated style), in which a single pitch is reiterated with rapid sixteenth notes. The second section, the final duet of the lovers Nero and Poppea, is an **A-B-B-A** pattern, a precursor to the da capo form **(A-B-A)** that will characterize Italian opera well into the eighteenth century. The **A** section features a four-note descending ground bass. In the recording, the basso continuo includes at various times a harpsichord, lute, and organ. In our recording, the role of Nero, originally a castrato, is sung by a mezzo-soprano, thus preserving the close dissonances Monteverdi wrote between the solo voices. Period instruments can also be heard in the three-part sinfonia that separates the two duets.

16

Henry Purcell

Dido and Aeneas, Act III, Dido's Lament and Chorus
(1689)

8CD: 1/ 52 – 55
4CD: 1/ 34 – 36

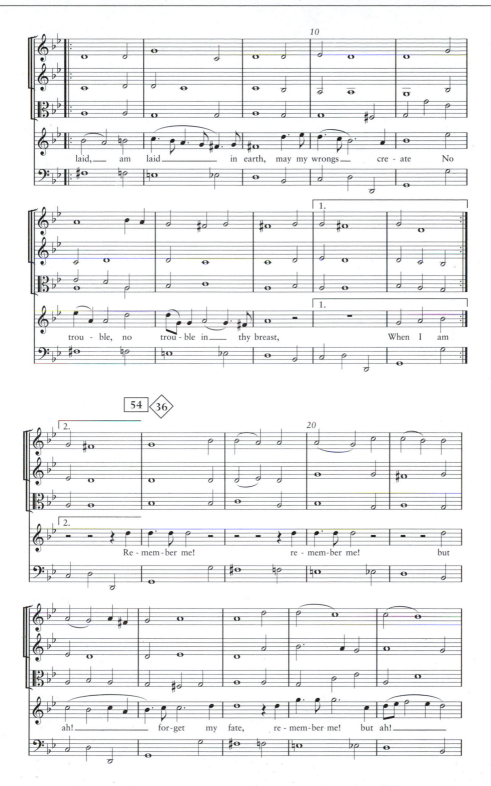

Dido and Aeneas, by Henry Purcell (1659–1695), is based on an episode in Virgil's *Aeneid*, in which the Trojan prince Aeneas pauses for a brief stay in Carthage, while on his journey to become the founder of Rome. He falls in love with the widowed Carthaginian queen Dido, but abandons her to fulfill his destiny. With his departure, Dido sings a final lament and dies in a burning funeral pyre. Since *Dido and Aeneas* was written for a performance at a boarding school for young women in 1689, the final "Remember me" would have been a clear moralizing message to the students.

After a brief recitative sung by Dido to her faithful serving maid Belinda, the aria begins with a chromatically descending ostinato theme in the bass. During the aria, the ground bass theme is heard eight times. The subtle overlapping of the phrases for the voice with the repetitions of the bass theme establishes a strong sense of continuity and creates numerous harmonic clashes that underscore Dido's pain. At the end of the aria, the orchestra repeats the theme twice more, with the addition of imitative chromatic descents in the upper strings.

As in the dramas of Ancient Greece, the chorus enters for a final comment at the close of the opera. The lament begins with a four-part point of imitation on a descending melodic line that emphasizes "drooping wings." Purcell provides additional word painting for "scattered" (a meandering melodic phrase) and "soft" (a sigh gesture). At the close, a homorhythmic texture reinforces the somber resolve of the final admonishment directed at the young audience.

17

George Frideric Handel

Rinaldo, Act I, Scene 1: Aria, "Molto voglio"
("I have great desires") (1711)

TEXT AND TRANSLATION

Molto voglio, molto spero,	I have great desires and great hopes,
nulla devo dubitar	I must doubt nothing.
(Molto voglio . . .)	(I have great desires . . .)
Di mia forza all'alto impero	With the strength of my imperial power,
Saprò il mondo assoggettar.	I will conquer the world.
(Molto voglio . . .)	(I have great desires . . .)

Rinaldo (1711) was Handel's first Italian opera written for London, where it remained one of his most popular works in the genre. Handel (1685–1759) would continue to compose and produce Italian operas in London for thirty years. The story of *Rinaldo*, set during the First Crusade (1096–1099), is taken from Torquato Tasso's epic *Gerusalemme liberata* (*Jerusalem Liberated*). By the end of the opera, Rinaldo helps liberate Jerusalem from the Muslims, outwits the sorceress Armida, and wins the hand of his beloved Almirena.

In Act I, Armida arrives in a chariot drawn by two dragons and delivers an impassioned aria expressing her ambitions. The da capo form (**A-B-A**) is standard for late Baroque Italian arias. The **A** section follows the typical structure: an opening ritornello; the initial presentation of the vocal melody (mm. 9–17); an intervening ritornello in the dominant key (mm. 17–19); the second portion of the vocal melody, ending in the tonic (mm. 19–27); and the closing ritornello (mm. 27–33). After the contrasting **B** section, which is accompanied by the basso continuo only (mm. 33–41), **A** is repeated with improvised embellishments, as can be heard on the recording.

Handel is economical in his use of melodic material for the **A** section. The opening ritornello contains four two-measure segments: the opening melody played by a solo oboe, a repeat of this melody by the orchestra, a rising flourish in the oboe, and the cadential material, which bears some similarities to the opening melody. The voice enters with a repetition of the opening ritornello theme and then moves to the dominant with a new idea featuring a distinctive repeating dotted rhythm. After the intervening ritornello, the voice launches into a melisma that recalls the oboe flourish, and then returns to the dotted-rhythm idea, now in the tonic (compare mm. 14–17 with mm. 23–27). These forceful dotted rhythms and vocal melismas, including the flourish on "assoggettar" ("conquer") in the **B** section, suggest that Armida is a powerful and dangerous character.

18

John Gay

The Beggar's Opera, end of Act II (1728)

8CD: 1/ 59 – 61

Air 38. "Why how now, Madam Flirt?"
(*Good-morrow, Gossip Joan*)

CUE: PEACHUM Sure all Women are alike! If ever they commit the Folly, they are sure to commit another by exposing themselves —
Away — Not a word more — You are my Prisoner now, Hussy.

Air 39. "No pow'r on earth"
(*Irish Howl*, by George Vanbrughe)

hoo____ hoo____ der-ry der-ry der-ry der-ry am – oo – ra.____ *(Holding Macheath, Peachum pulling her)*

CUE: MACHEATH A Moment of time may make us unhappy forever.

Air 40. "I like the Fox shall grieve"
(*The Lass of Patie's Mill*)

Version A

LUCY I like the Fox shall grieve,____ Whose mate hath_ left_ her_ side, Whom

Hounds, from morn to eve,____ Chase o'er____ the coun – try wide.

Where_ can my_ lo – ver hide? Where cheat____ the wea – ry____

Editor's note: Because of a weak bass part in this piece (given as Version A here), the editor, Jeremy Barlow, prepared an alternative version from another eighteenth-century source (Version B), which is performed on the Norton recording.

With *The Beggar's Opera*, John Gay (1685–1732) established a new tradition for the ballad opera that would enjoy widespread popularity. Following a simple formula, Gay inserted a number of songs into a spoken comedic play. The songs were not original, but were borrowed from a variety of sources, generally popular, with the words changed to meet the needs of the play. For the most part, the tunes are simple, short, and accompanied by basso continuo or small ensemble.

The end of Act II contains three contrasting songs. Air 38 is a delightful strophic duet. Lucy and Polly take turns taunting each other with a twelve-measure tune embellished lightly with operatic flourishes. Air 39, in which Polly sings of her love for Macheath, is a simple **A-A-B-C** tune that reaches its highest point in the last phrase. The close on the dominant suggests the staging, as her father is pulling her away. The act closes with a sentimental melody, Air 40, in which Lucy acknowledges that by helping Macheath, she will never see him again. The binary form of the melody suggests a dance conception for the original tune.

19

Barbara Strozzi

Cantata, *Begli occhi* (*Beautiful Eyes*) (published 1654)

8CD: 1/ 62 – 67
4CD: 1/ 37 – 42

TEXT AND TRANSLATION

Mi ferite oh begli occhi.	You wound me, oh beautiful eyes.
Pensate che farebbono quei baci	Imagine what these kisses could do
si concenti e mordaci.	so burning and biting
Langue l'anima e il cor vien meno	My soul languishes and my heart faints:
Ahi ch'io vi moro in seno!	Oh that I die there in my breast!
Pensate che farebbono gli strali;	Imagine what arrows could do;
si pungente e mortali.	so sharp and deadly.
Langue l'anima e il cor vien meno	My soul languishes and my heart faints:
ahi ch'io vi moro in seno!	Oh that I die there in my breast!
Ma forse non morrò senza vendetta;	But perhaps I will not die without revenge;
ch'al fin chi morte da, la morte aspetta!	For he who deals death, awaits it in the end!

One of the musical innovations of the early Baroque period was a new vocal style called *monody*. Inspired by descriptions of Greek music, monody features an expressive solo melody with simple chordal accompaniment. Two distinct melodic styles can be observed in the monodies of the early seventeenth century: a freer, more expressive style similar to recitative and a more tuneful aria style. Both can be found in dramatic works (operas), sacred music, and in extended secular songs, which became known as *cantatas*. The accompaniment for monodies, played by a melodic bass instrument and an instrument capable of improvising chords from a figured bass line, is called the *basso continuo*. In the recording, the basso continuo is played by a cello and a harpsichord.

Begli occhi (*Beautiful Eyes*), by Barbara Strozzi (1619–1677), is a secular cantata published in 1654 for two high solo voices and basso continuo, a common texture in the Baroque era. Typical of the time, the cantata contains both recitative and aria styles. Three aria-like passages in triple meter can be heard: the two settings of the lines beginning with the word "pensate" (mm. 12 and 38) and the final duplet (m. 66). The other melodic material, set with a freer rhythmic pulse, tends to be more chromatic and dissonant. Particularly striking is the word painting for "Langue l'anima" ("my soul languishes"), which involves chromaticism and half-step movement. The end of the cantata presents a virtuosic display in the upper voices, as the poem closes with a delightful example of word painting (a lengthy melisma on "aspetta," suggesting the long wait for death) and visions of eternal retribution.

20

Johann Sebastian Bach

Cantata No. 80, *Ein feste Burg ist unser Gott*
(*A Mighty Fortress Is Our God*), excerpts (1715/c. 1744)

8CD: 2/ 1 – 13
4CD: 1/ 43 – 51

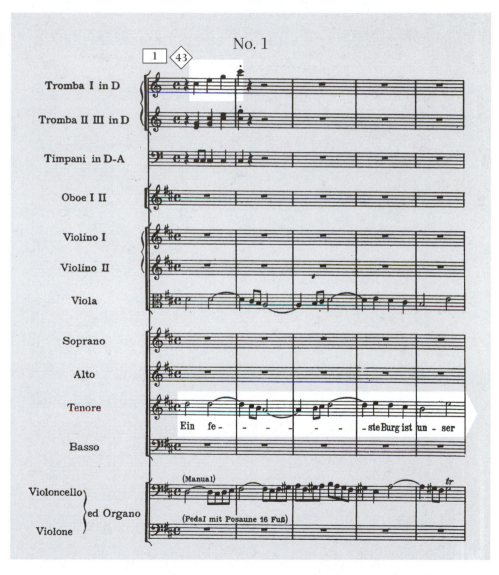

Editor's note: Trumpets and timpani were added by Wilhelm Friedemann Bach. The chorale tune, set in **A-A-B** form, is in its original version in the top line of movement 8 of this cantata (see p. 162).

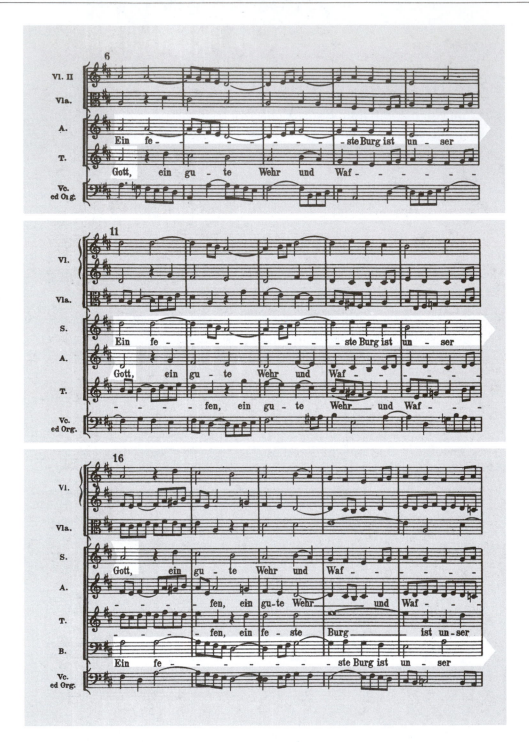

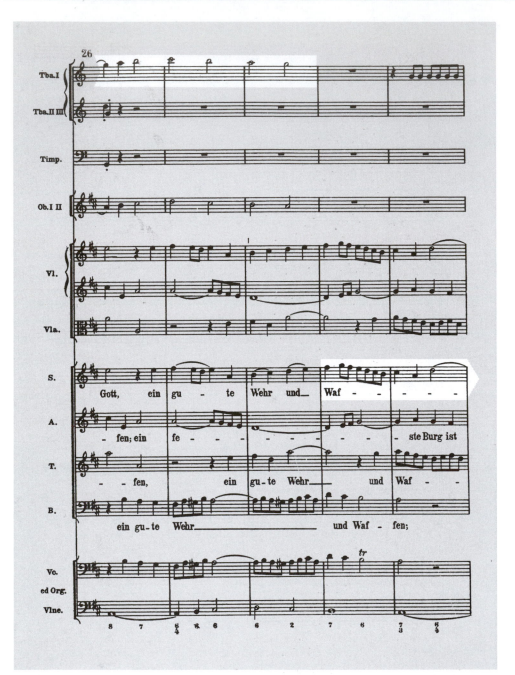

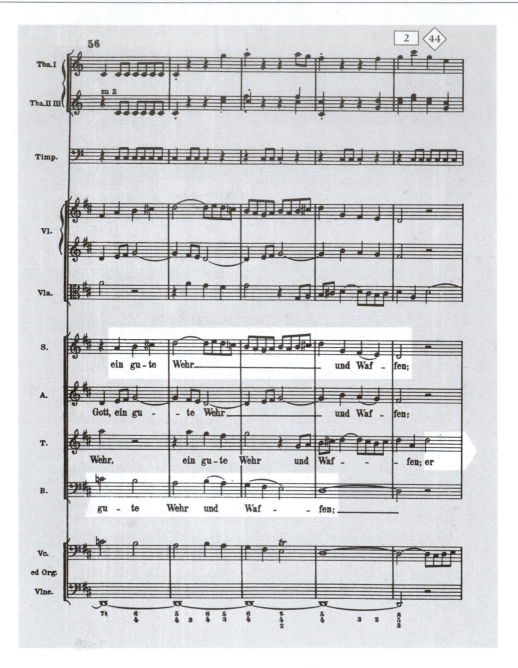

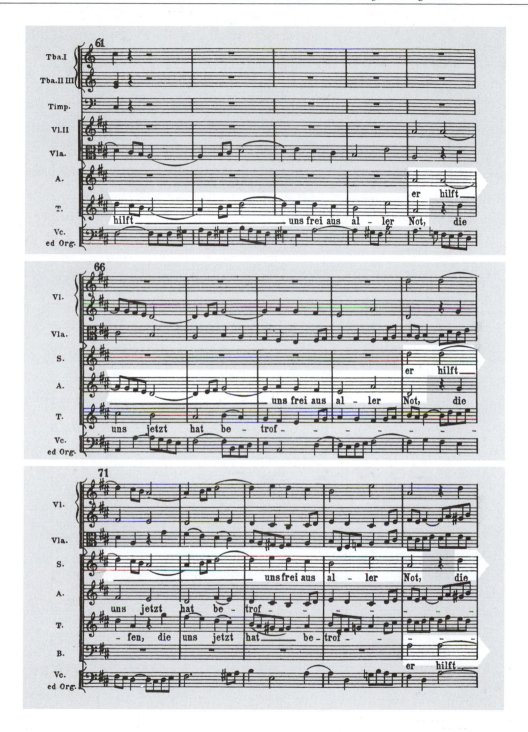

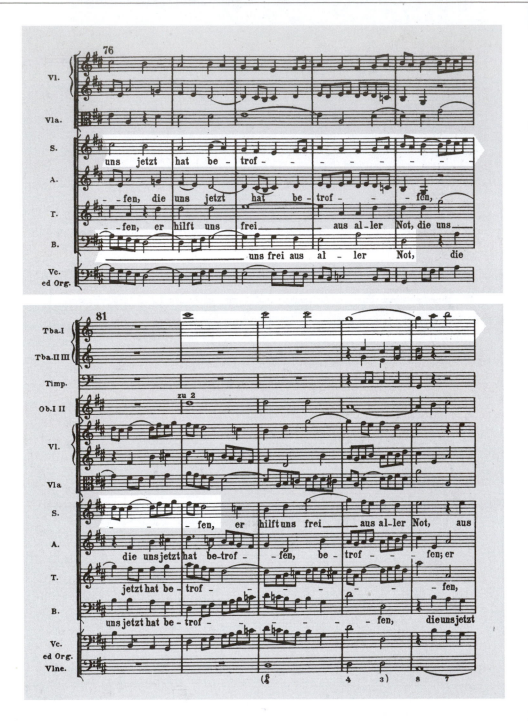

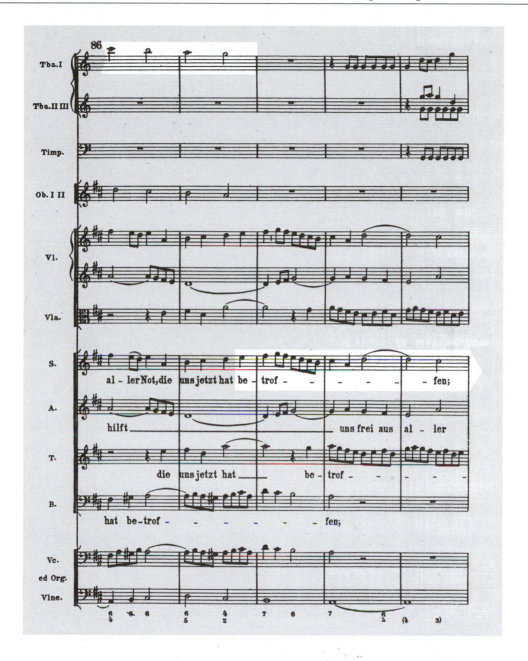

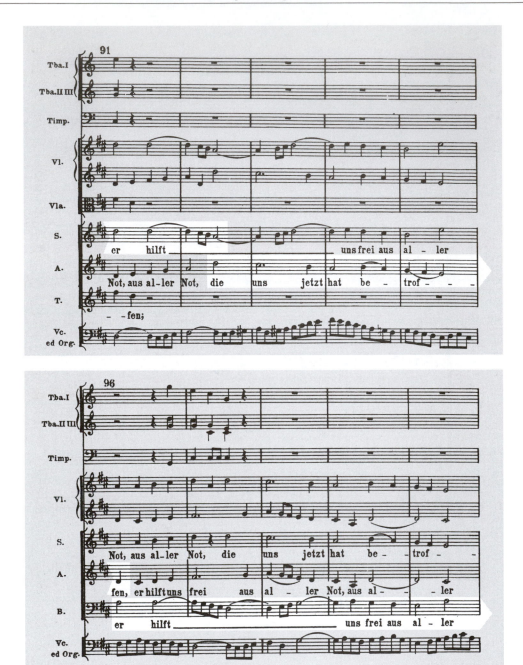

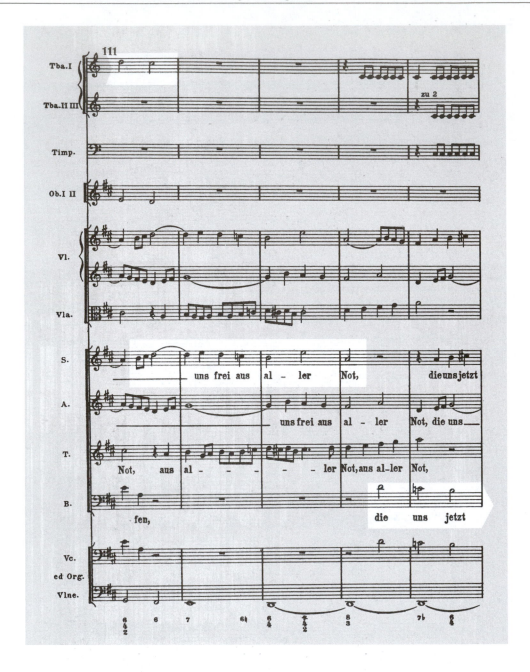

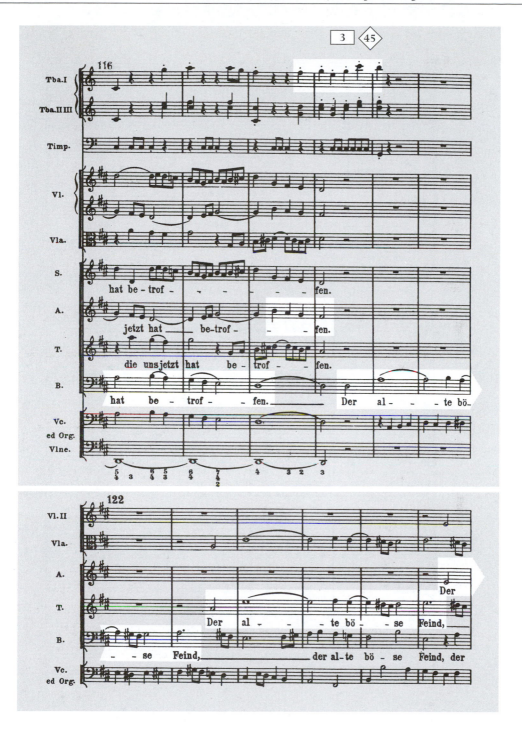

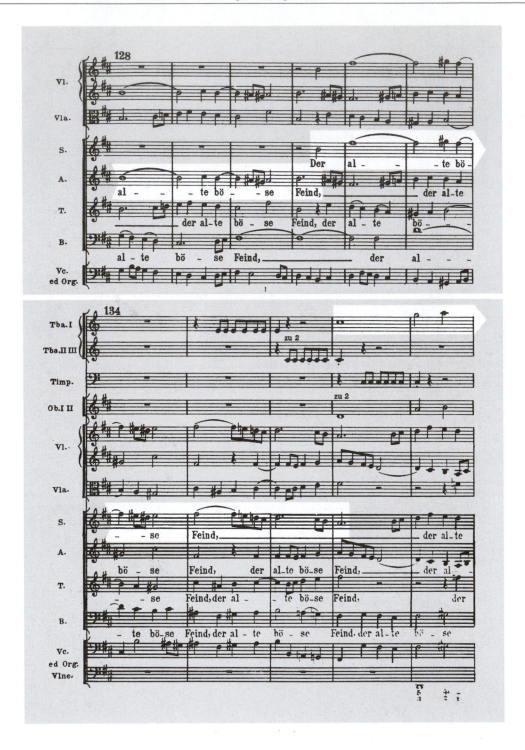

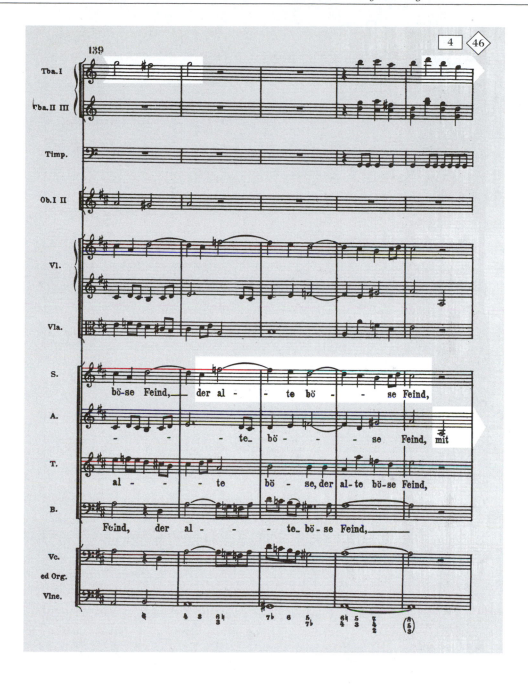

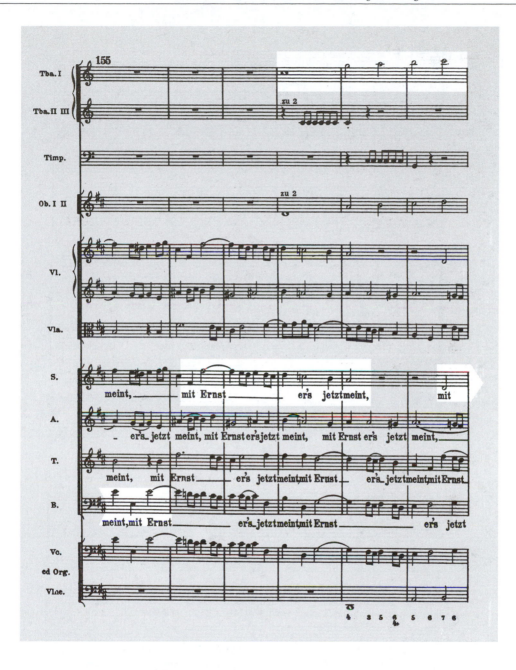

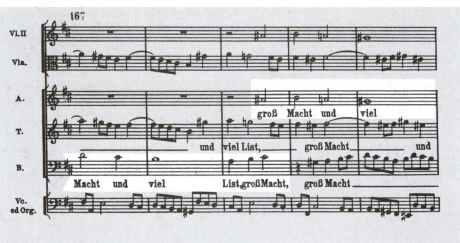

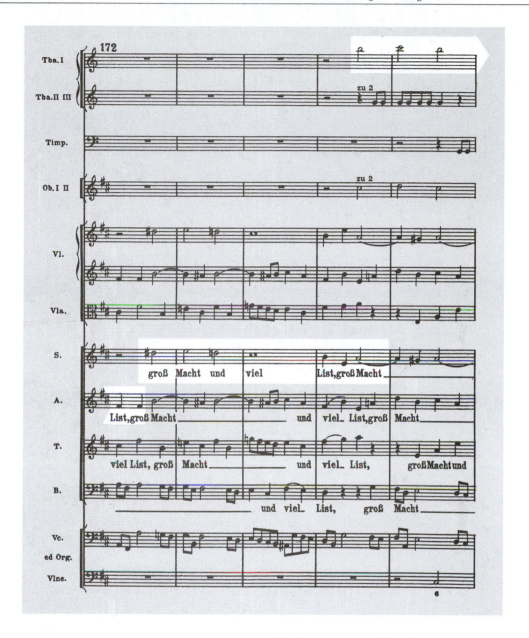

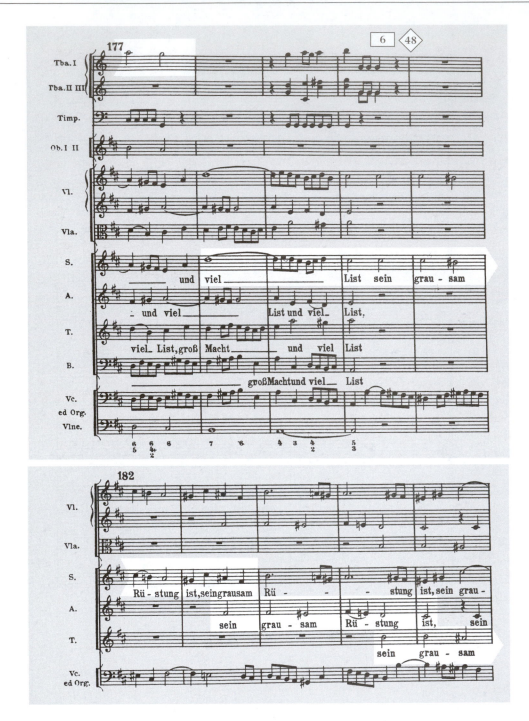

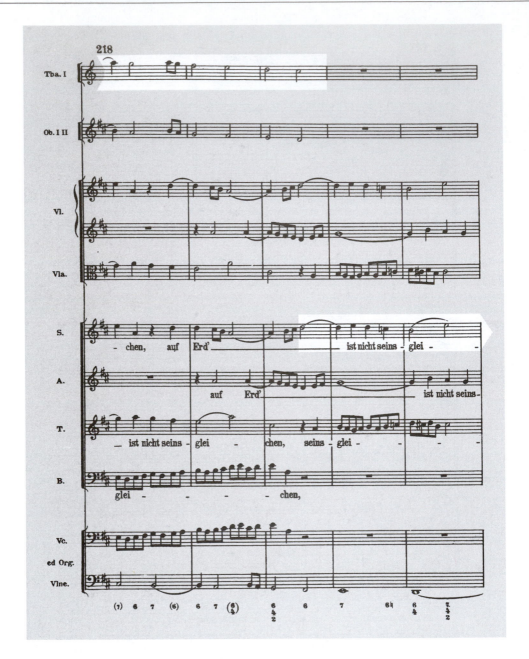

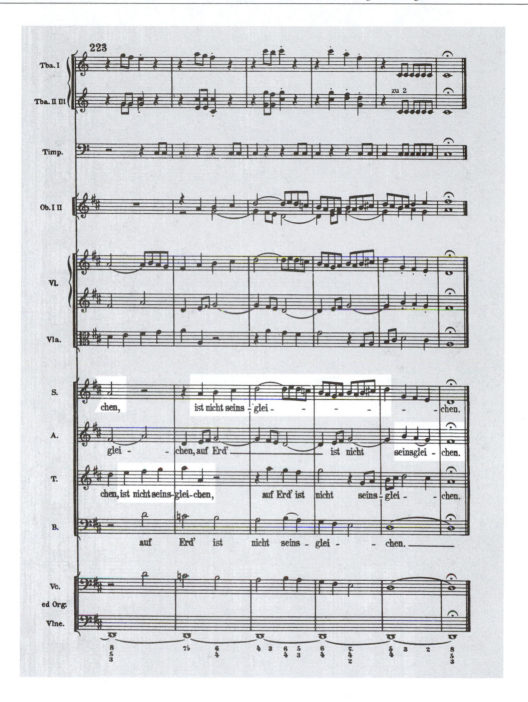

No. 5

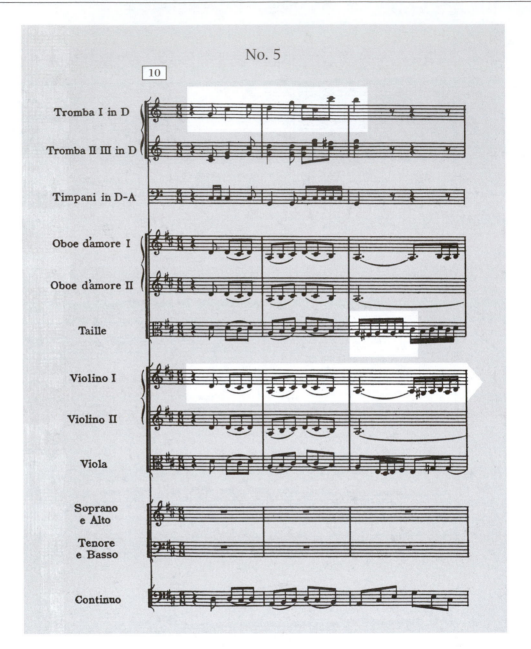

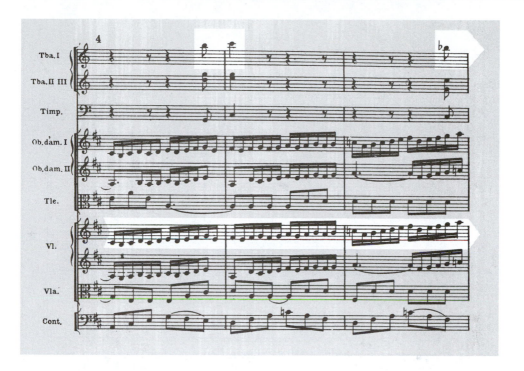

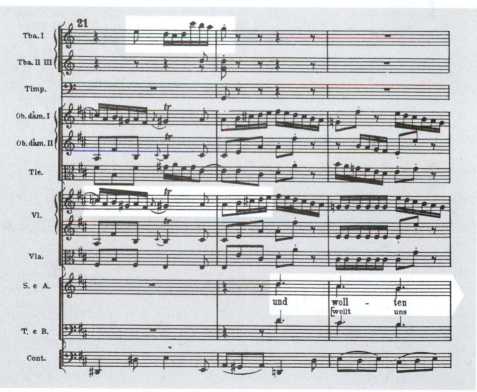

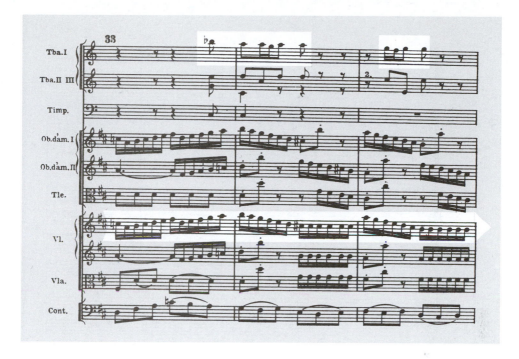

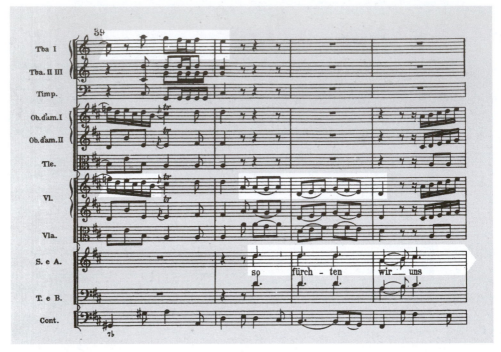

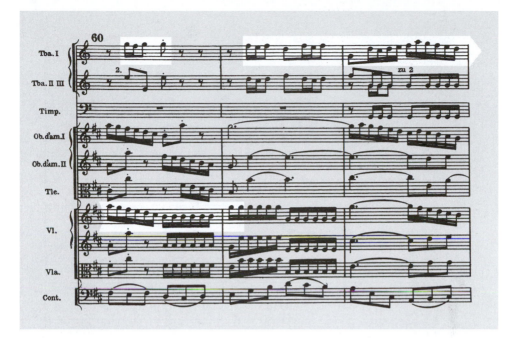

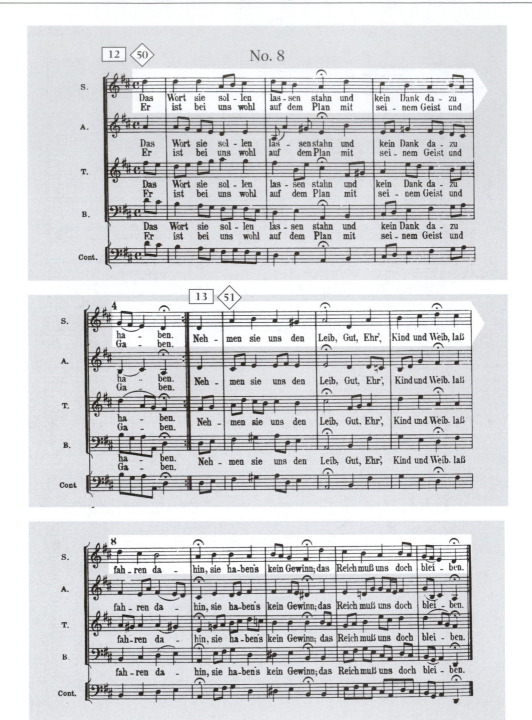

TEXT AND TRANSLATION

1. Choral Fugue

Ein feste Burg ist unser Gott,
ein' gute Wehr und Waffen;
er hilft uns frei aus aller Not,
die uns jetzt hat betroffen.

Der alte böse Feind,
mit Ernst er's jetzt meint,
gross Macht und viel List;
sein grausam Rüstung ist;
auf Erd' ist nicht seinsgleichen.

A mighty fortress is our God,
a good defense and weapon;
He helps free us from all the troubles
that have now befallen us.

Our ever evil foe,
in earnest plots against us,
with great strength and cunning
he prepares his dreadful plans.
Earth holds none like him.

2. Duet

Soprano

Mit unser Macht ist nichts getan,
wir sind gar bald verloren.
Es streit't für uns der rechte Mann,
den Gott selbst hat erkoren.

Fragst du, wer er ist?
Er heisst Jesus Christ,
der Herre Zebaoth,
und ist kein andrer Gott,
das Feld muss er behalten.

With our own strength nothing is achieved,
we would soon be lost.
But on our behalf strives the Mighty One,
whom God Himself has chosen.

Ask you, who is he?
He is called Jesus Christ,
Lord of Hosts,
And there is no other God,
He must remain master of the field.

Bass

Alles was von Gott geboren,
ist zum Siegen auserkoren.
Wer bei Christi Blutpanier
in der Taufe Treu' geschworen,
siegt im Geiste für und für.

Everything born of God
has been chosen for victory.
He who holds to Christ's banner,
truly sworn in baptism,
his spirit will conquer forever and ever.

5. Chorus

Und wenn die Welt voll Teufel wär
und wollten uns verschlingen,
so fürchten wir uns nicht so sehr,
es soll uns doch gelingen.

Der Fürst dieser Welt,
wie saur er sich stellt,
tut er uns doch nicht,
das macht, er ist gericht't,
ein Wörtlein kann ihn fällen.

Though the world were full of devils
eager to devour us,
we need have no fear,
as we will still prevail.

The arch-fiend of this world,
no matter how bitter his stand,
cannot harm us,
indeed he faces judgment,
one Word from God will bring him low.

8. Chorale

Das Wort sie sollen lassen stahn	Now let the Word of God abide
und kein Dank dazu haben.	without further thought.
Er ist bei uns wohl auf dem Plan	He is firmly on our side
mit seinem Geist und Gaben.	with His spirit and strength.
Nehmen sie uns den Leib,	Though they deprive us of life,
Gut, Ehr', Kind, und Weib,	wealth, honor, child, and wife,
lass fahren dahin,	we will not complain,
sie haben's kein Gewinn;	it will avail them nothing;
das Reich muss uns doch bleiben.	for God's kingdom must prevail.

In his positions with several Lutheran churches, and particularly as cantor of St. Thomas's in Leipzig, Bach composed over two-hundred cantatas. His cantata *Ein feste Burg ist unser Gott* (*A Mighty Fortress Is Our God*) was originally written in Weimar for performance during Lent. Since cantatas were not performed during Lent in Leipzig, Bach adapted the cantata for the Feast of the Reformation (October 31), which commemorates the day that Martin Luther posted his ninety-five theses in 1517.

Bach frequently incorporated chorale tunes in his sacred works, and his Cantata No. 80 features the chorale *Ein feste Burg ist unser Gott*, attributed to Martin Luther himself. In its final version, the cantata contains eight movements, and the chorale appears in movements 1, 2, 5, and 8. The other movements are recitatives and arias for solo singers. Typical of Bach, the most elaborate setting of the chorale melody is in the opening movement. Bach retains the original bar form of the tune (**A-A-B**) and subdivides the **A** section into two phrases and the **B** section into five phrases. Each phrase of the chorale tune is heard in the oboes and trumpets. Preceding these statements are choral fugues based on the individual chorale phrases.

The second movement sets the tune in a four-part texture. The accompanying parts consist of a perpetual-motion unison string line, a walking bass line, and a virtuoso solo bass melody. The solo soprano and oboes present an ornamented version of the tune, sometimes in a heterophonic texture. In the fifth movement, a unison choir intones the chorale, while the orchestra plays an elaborate accompaniment. The simplest presentation of the tune is in the final movement, where the entire congregation would have joined in singing the melody. The chorale is set in a simple, homophonic, four-part texture, with the melody in the top voice.

21

George Frideric Handel

Oratorio, *Messiah*, excerpts (1742)

8CD: 2/ 14 – 25
4CD: 1/⟨52⟩ – ⟨57⟩

Overture

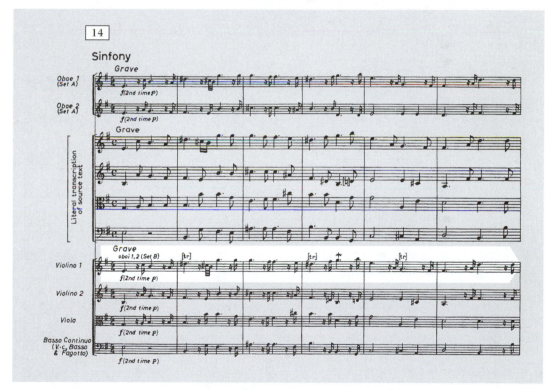

Editor's note: This edition shows the Grave as notated (with simple dotted rhythms) and as played following the Baroque performance practice of rhythmic alteration (resulting in double dotted rhythms). The indication of Sets A and B in the oboe parts refer to variant manuscript sources.

* Except where specifically marked 'violoncello' by the composer, passages in the *basso continuo* written in the C clefs are treated in this edition as *bassetti* and are not included in the bassoon and cello-bass orchestral parts, unless specially noted, as here.

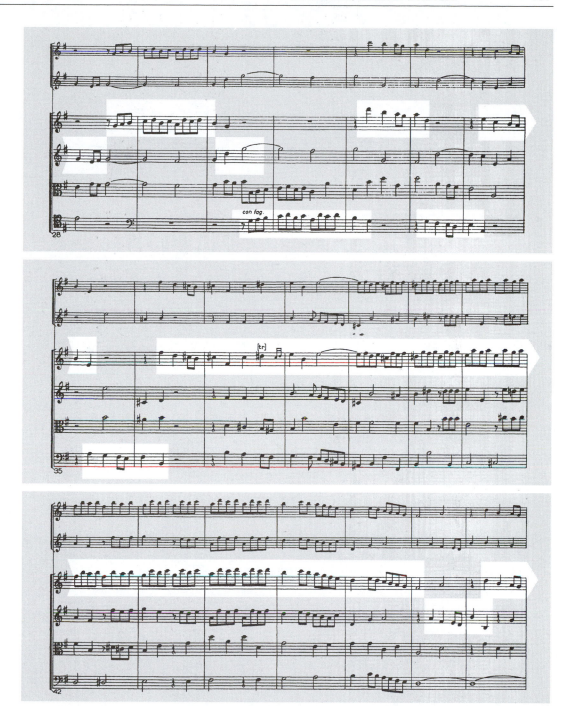

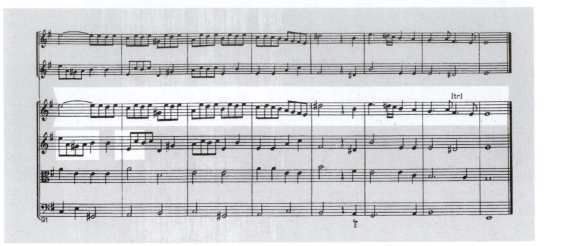

No. 14a Recitative *(secco)*: THERE WERE SHEPHERDS ABIDING IN THE FIELD

Luke ii, 8

No. 14b Recitative *(accompagnato)*: AND, LO, THE ANGEL OF THE LORD CAME UPON THEM

Luke ii, 9

No. 15   Recitative *(secco)*: AND THE ANGEL SAID UNTO THEM

Luke ii, 10–11

No. 16   Recitative *(accompagnato)*: AND SUDDENLY THERE WAS WITH THE ANGEL

Luke ii, 13

No. 17 Chorus: GLORY TO GOD

No. 18 Aria: REJOICE GREATLY, O DAUGHTER OF ZION

Zechariah ix, 9–10

Editor's note: Tempo, dynamic markings, trills, and other performance markings in square brackets are editorial. Alternate rhythms reflecting the Baroque performance practice of rhythmic alteration appear above the music.

*Grace notes from the Autograph.

No. 44 Chorus: "HALLELUJAH"

Editor's note: Square brackets are used in the accompaniment to show the end of a passage for a particular instrument or instruments; text is set in capital letters where it was lacking or abbreviated in the original source.

* Alto: Handel himself wrote both notes.

Handel's oratorio *Messiah* (1742) can be seen as a mixture of the Baroque Italian operatic style and the English choral tradition. The overture, however, is fashioned after the model created by Jean-Baptiste Lully in France, commonly known as the French overture. Set in a rounded binary form, the slow tempo, minor key, and dotted rhythms of the opening section create a stately, somber character. The second half of the overture, set in a quicker tempo, features a fugal texture and never strays too far from the home key of E minor. In a performance tradition of French overtures known as overdotting, the dotted rhythms in the slower tempo are altered, so that the dotted quarter notes are lengthened and the eighth notes are shortened.

The Italian opera style can best be heard in the sections for solo voices. Following the Italian tradition, recitatives and arias are clearly separated. The predominant *secco* style of Italian recitative can be heard at the beginning of numbers 14a ⟨9⟩ and 15 ⟨10⟩, and both are followed by *recitative accompagnato* passages in which the texts refer to images of angels. The soprano aria "Rejoice greatly, O daughter of Zion" reflects the Italian predilection for virtuosity and ornamentation, especially in the setting of the word "rejoice." The **A-B-A** form suggests a *da capo* structure, but the opening **A** section closes in the dominant rather than the tonic, thereby negating the possibility of a literal da capo repeat, and the reprise of **A** is truncated.

Handel's mastery of the choral style is clearly evident in the contrasting movements "Glory to God" and the "Hallelujah Chorus." "Glory to God" is a succinct and energetic setting in which the music vividly supports the meaning of the text. In the "Hallelujah Chorus," Handel manipulates a variety of textures to build dramatic tension. At the beginning, he juxtaposes a chordal setting of the word "Hallelujah!" with the monophonic phrase "for the Lord God omnipotent reigneth," and then combines the two in excited counterpoint. The climax of the chorus occurs with the intoning of "King of Kings," punctuated with trumpet, timpani, and the full orchestra.

22

Arcangelo Corelli

Trio Sonata, Op. 3, No. 2, Third and Fourth movements
(published 1689)

8CD: 2/ 26 – 28

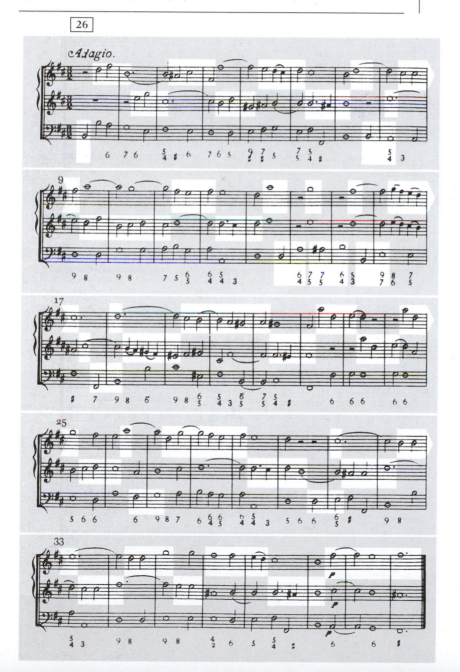

The trio sonata was one of the most common instrumental genres of the Baroque era. Primarily performed with two violins and a basso continuo (a cello with either a harpsichord or organ), these sonatas are set either as a series of dance movements (*sonata da camera*) or in a four-movement pattern of slow-fast-slow-fast (*sonata da chiesa*). Arcangelo Corelli (1653–1713), with four publications of twelve trio sonatas in each, can be seen as the foremost composer of the genre.

These two movements from his Op. 3, No. 2, are the second half of a *sonata da chiesa* structure. The Adagio exhibits the tempo and rhythmic gestures of a sarabande dance, but the form is continuous. While the upper voices alternate passages in imitation, parallel thirds, and chains of suspensions, the bass line primarily serves a harmonic function. The final cadence, offset with a hemiola, closes on the dominant of B minor and is never resolved, as the Allegro begins in D major.

The Allegro also suggests a dance rhythm—the gigue—and it is set in the standard binary form of the Baroque dance. A three-part fugal texture involving an active bass line can be heard throughout the movement. The second half begins with an inverted statement of the principal subject. The period instruments heard in the recording clearly delineate each line and create a warm, homogenous sound.

23

Domenico Scarlatti

Sonata in C major, K. 159 (*La Caccia*) (*The Hunt*) (1738)

Domenico Scarlatti (1658–1757), one of Italy's finest keyboard composers, spent most of his career in Portugal and Spain. Living in relative isolation, Scarlatti developed a unique keyboard style that featured colorful invocations of Spanish music, bold harmonies, an idiomatic keyboard technique, and a rounded binary form that shares numerous characteristics with sonata-allegro form. He completed over 550 sonatas for harpsichord, many of which have only a single movement. Thirty sonatas were published in 1738 under the title *Essercizi* (exercises).

The Sonata in C major illustrates Scarlatti's creative approach to keyboard music. The work's subtitle, *La Caccia* (*The Hunt*), is reflected in the quick tempo, compound meter, and hunting-call motives. Ornaments (grace notes and trills), repeated pitches, and biting dissonances on downbeats contribute to the Spanish character of the work. The music of the **B** section even mimics the sound of a strummed guitar and castanets, instruments of Spanish flamenco dancing.

The structure resembles a sonata-allegro form in its overall design; the **A** section moves from tonic to dominant, the beginning of the **B** section is harmonically unstable, and there is a strong sense of return at measure 43 following a brief dominant flourish. Although there is no "second theme" marking the arrival of the dominant, as there would be in a sonata-allegro, the material in the dominant section of **A** does return at the end of **B** in the tonic.

24

Johann Sebastian Bach

Contrapunctus 1, from *The Art of Fugue* (published 1751)

8CD: 2/ 31 – 34
4CD: 1/ 58 – 61

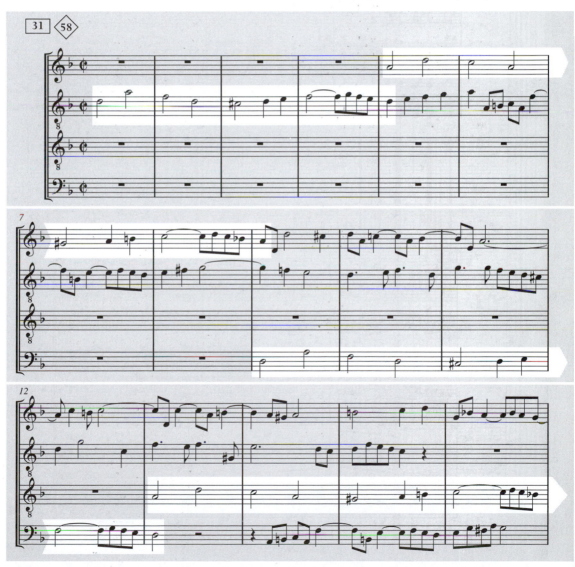

Editor's note: In this work, only complete statements of the theme (subject and answer) are highlighted.

The Art of Fugue, Bach's last major work, was published posthumously in 1751. A compendium of contrapuntal devices, the collection contains fourteen fugues and four canons. Because the four lines are written on individual staves, a variety of instrumental combinations can play the work. Yet scholarly research seems to suggest that a performance by either organ or harpsichord was intended.

Contrapunctus I introduces the principal theme of the collection in a four-part fugue. During the exposition (mm. 1–16), the subject (in the alto and bass) and answer forms (in the soprano and tenor) of the theme alternate. There is no distinct countersubject, but the motives in the accompanying lines combine with those from the theme to generate the bulk of the material for the fugue. Following the first episode (mm. 17–22), three additional entrances of the complete theme appear in the tonic key (m. 23 alto, m. 29 soprano, and m. 32 bass). The last two statements overlap, creating a stretto.

The middle portion of the fugue contains more extended episodes and two entries in the dominant (m. 40 alto and m. 49 soprano). The tonic key returns dramatically at measure 56 with a statement of the theme in the bass voice. Bach signals the imminent end of the fugue with a dominant pedal (m. 63), an intense drive to a climactic diminished-seventh chord (m. 70), two abrupt rests, and a final tonic pedal with a last thematic statement in the tenor (m. 74). As is typical of Baroque fugal writing, most of the thematic entrances are preceded by rests and sometimes by false entrances in other voices.

25

Antonio Vivaldi

La primavera, from *Le quattro stagioni*
(*Spring,* from *The Four Seasons*) (published 1725)

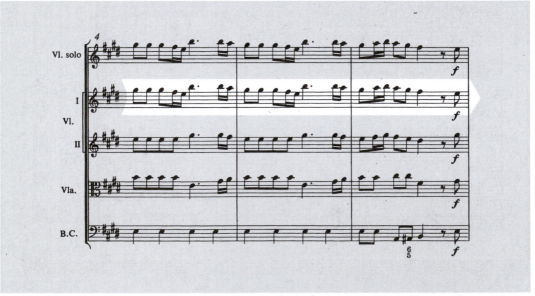

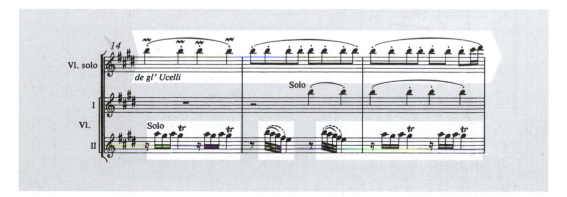

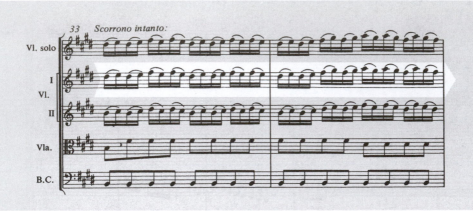

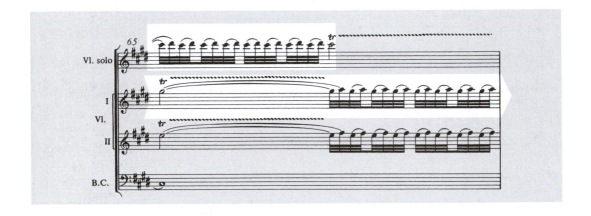

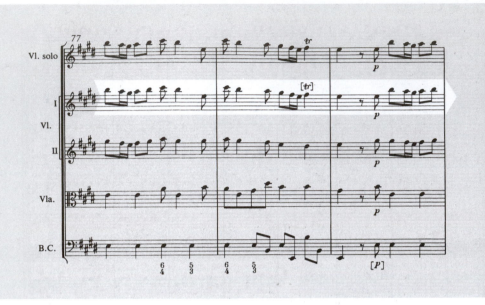

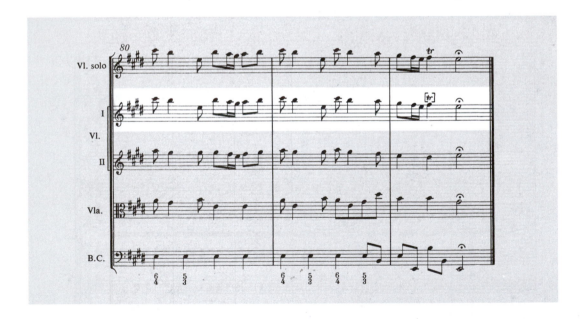

II

Editor's note: The continuation of the dotted pattern in measure 1 in Violin 1 and 2 is implied (usually marked simile). The viola instructions translate: "this should always be played very loud and strongly accented."

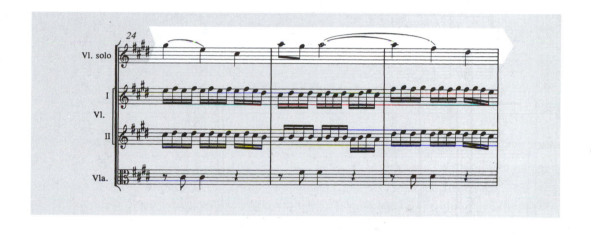

III

DANZA PASTORALE

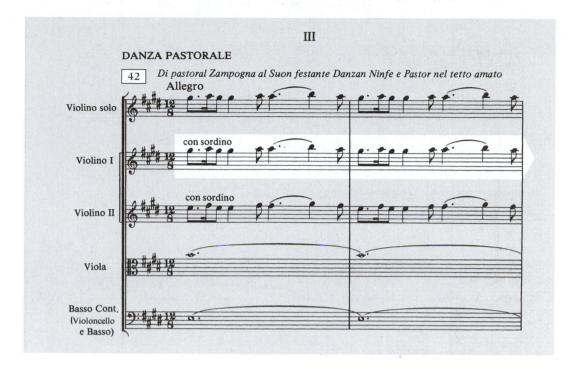

Di pastoral Zampogna al Suon festante Danzan Ninfe e Pastor nel tetto amato

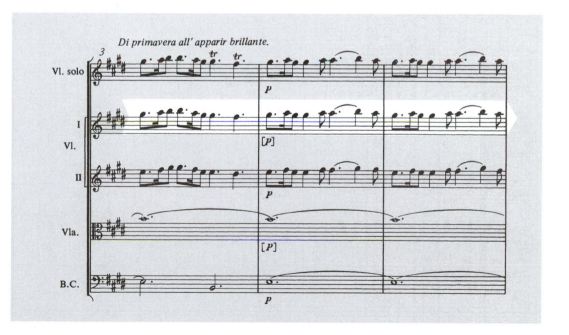

TEXT AND TRANSLATION

I. Allegro

Giunt' è la Primavera e festosetti
la salutan gl'augei con lieto canto,
e i fonti allo spirar de'zeffiretti
con dolce mormorio scorrono intanto.

Vengon' coprendo l'aer di nero amanto,
e lampi, e tuoni ad annuntiarla eletti.
Indi tacendo questi, gl'augeletti;
tornan' di nuovo allor canoro incanto.

Joyful spring has arrived,
the birds greet it with their cheerful song,
and the brooks in the gentle breezes
flow with a sweet murmur.

The sky is covered with a black mantle,
and thunder and lightning announce a storm.
When they fall silent, the birds
take up again their melodious song.

II. Largo

E quindi sul fiorito ameno prato,
Al caro mormorio di fronde e piante,
Dorme'l caprar col fido can'a lato.

And in the pleasant, flowery meadow,
to the gentle murmur of bushes and trees,
the goatherd sleeps, with his faithful dog at
  his side.

III. Allegro (Rustic Dance)

Di pastoral zampogna al suon festante
danzan ninfe e pastor nel tetto amato

di primavera all'apparir brillante.

To the festive sounds of a rustic bagpipe
nymphs and shepherd dance in their
  favorite spot
when spring appears in its brilliance.

Le quattro stagioni (The Four Seasons) of Antonio Vivaldi (1678–1741) are
his most celebrated violin concertos. Published in 1725 as Op. 8, Nos. 1–4,
these programmatic concertos depict scenes in each of the seasons of the
year. Interpolated onto the score of each concerto is a sonnet (presumably
by Vivaldi) describing the particular season.

In *La primavera (Spring)*, the poem avoids any sense of narrative and is limited to general visions of spring. These pictorial images are presented within
the framework of the solo violin concerto as established by Vivaldi. In addition to the three-movement format, the outer allegro movements retain ritornello structures. In the first movement, the orchestral ritornello statements
are separated by episodes (often featuring a virtuoso solo violin part) that
depict the sounds of birds, a murmuring brook, a storm, and birds again. The
slow movement features a cantabile solo violin melody, which is performed

with improvised embellishments in the recording. The warmth of tone created by the gut strings and Baroque bow enhances the tranquil mood. The orchestral accompaniment, which omits the lower strings and harpsichord continuo, is characterized by a repetitive dotted rhythm in the violins and a two-note figure in the violas that represents a barking dog. The dancelike ritornello theme of the third movement is set over a bagpipe-like drone in the lower strings. The orchestra ritornello and the solo sections, revealing a variety of solo/orchestra relationships, sustain the general image of joyful dancing. The period instruments heard in the recording create a clearly articulated sound that is particularly effective in passages with rapid notes, such as in the depiction of lightning and the subsequent flight of birds.

26

Johann Sebastian Bach

Brandenburg Concerto No. 2 in F major, First movement
(1717–18)

8CD: 2/ 43 – 47

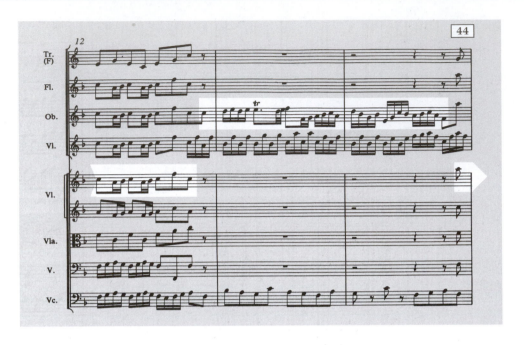

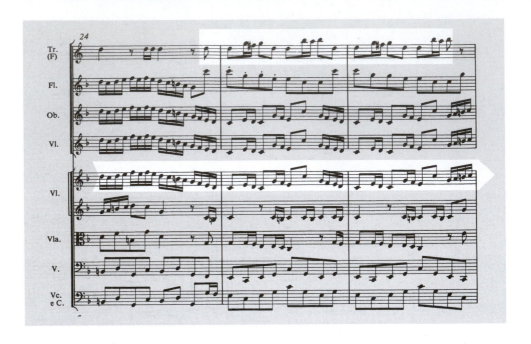

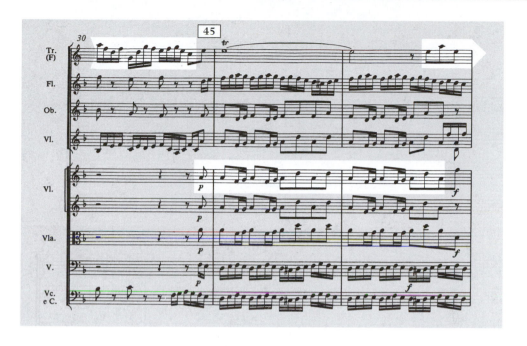

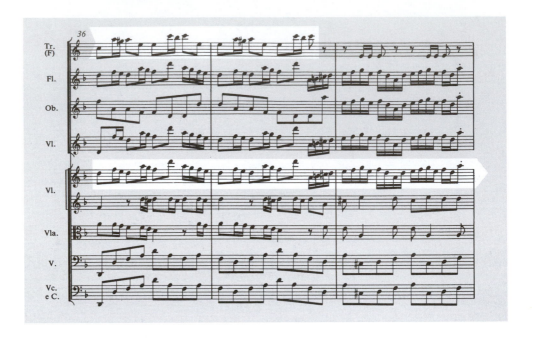

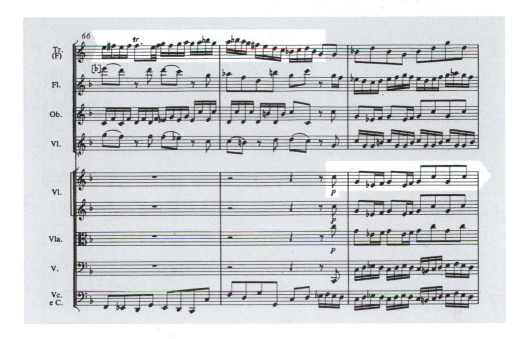

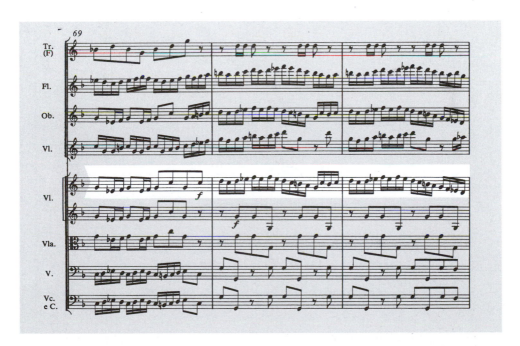

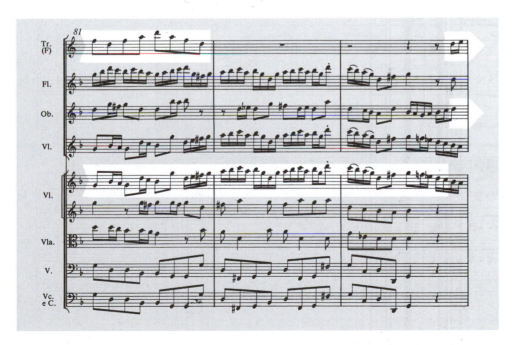

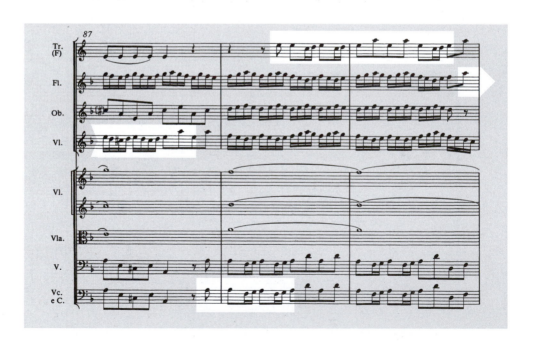

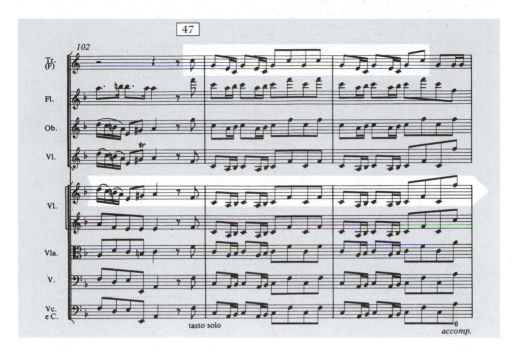

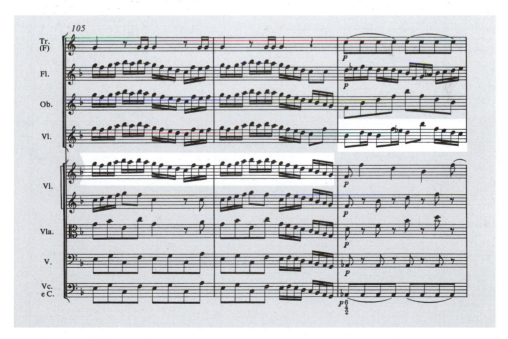

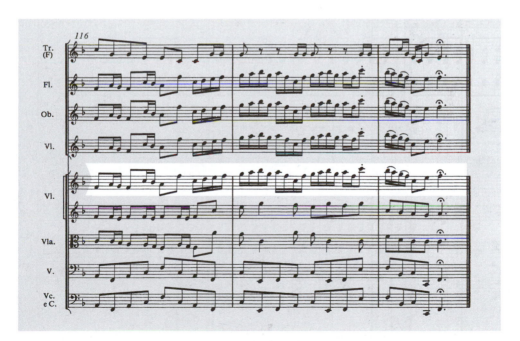

The second of Bach's six concertos dedicated to the margrave of Brandenburg (1717–18) is written for an unusual group of soloists (*concertino*)—violin, oboe, recorder, and trumpet—and a *tutti* string orchestra (*ripieno*) that includes a cello and harpsichord continuo. Although the work maintains ties to the traditions of the concerto grosso, it also exhibits the virtuosity and structure of the solo concerto, including its three-movement format.

As in a Vivaldi solo concerto, the first movement is in ritornello form, and the *tutti* statements help define tonal areas in the closely related major and minor keys. But the prominence of the orchestra during the solo sections and the frequent contrapuntal texture create a more complicated structure than that found in Vivaldi's works.

27

George Frideric Handel

Water Music, Suite in D major,
Allegro and Alla hornpipe (1717)

8CD: 2/ 48 – 53
4CD: 2/ 1 – 3

Allegro

Editor's note: In the Norton recording, timpani have been added. In the Baroque era, the timpani functioned as the bass of the trumpet family.

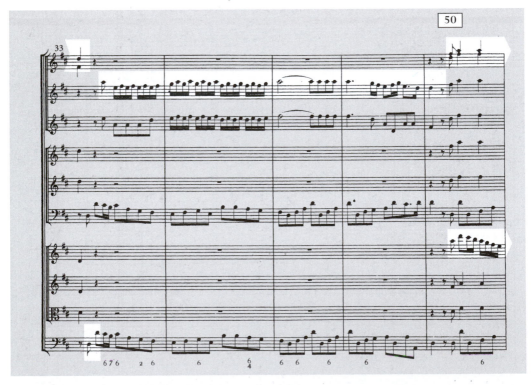

Alla hornpipe

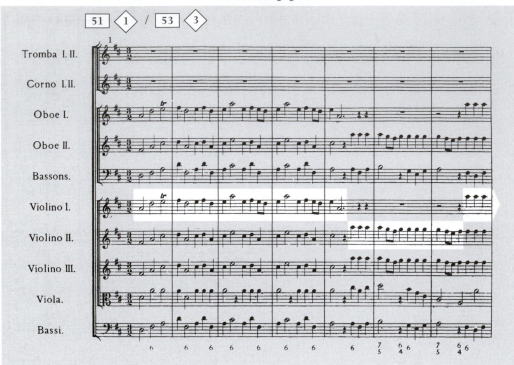

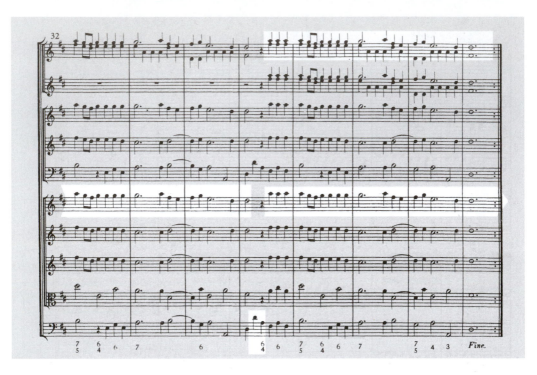

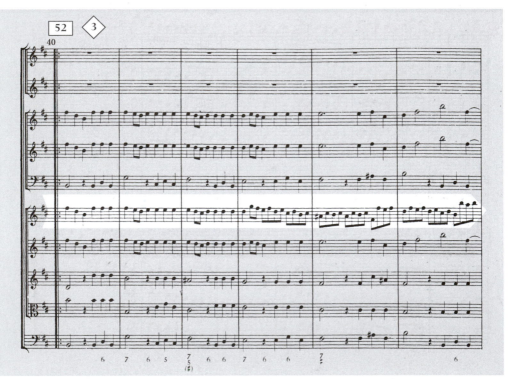

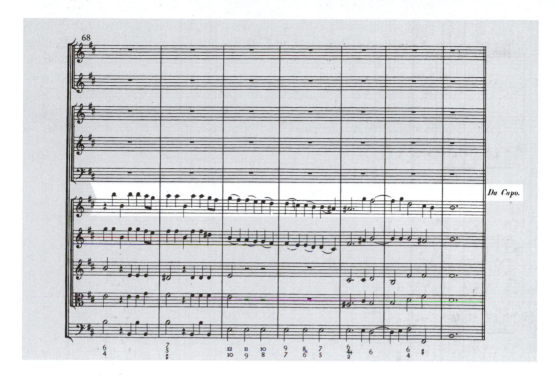

The two orchestral suites by George Frideric Handel (1685–1759) are festive pieces intended for outdoor performance. Indeed, *Water Music* (1717) may have been performed on the Thames River, with the musicians on barges providing entertainment for a royal party. The music is unusual in several respects. The traditional order of the suite is abandoned, the continuo part is omitted, and many of the movements, including the two featured in this anthology, avoid the pervasive binary form found in the standard dance suite.

In the Allegro, a series of thematic ideas, extending from two notes to four measures in length, is presented with alternating timbres. The trumpets, accompanied by unison violins, violas, and oboes, initiate the thematic ideas; the horns, accompanied by unison cellos, basses, and bassoons, repeat the material in a lower register. Ultimately, the two groups join forces (m. 38) when the opening phrase returns. In this recording with period instruments, the sound of the valveless brass instruments is striking. Because of their dependency on the natural series of overtones, the brass instruments can only play conjunct melodic material in their higher registers. In keeping with performance practices, a timpani part has been added as a bass for the trumpet family, and during the three-measure transition (Adagio) that separates the two movements, a violinist links the chords with an improvised cadenza.

The hornpipe, set in the standard 3/2 meter associated with the dance, has a ternary (**A-B-A**) form. The **B** section provides a strong contrast by moving from the tonic to B minor. This section features an extended eighth-note passage played by the first violin section that is particularly effective with period instruments. Although this material is new, the accompaniment, with its three quarter-note pick-ups, links the middle section to the second thematic idea of the **A** section.

28

Jean-Joseph Mouret

Rondeau, from *Suite de symphonies* (1729)

Editors note: The performance on the Norton recording, on modern instruments, differs slightly from the original in rhythmic interpretation (using overdotting in timpani) and choice of instruments. In the figured bass, a 5 indicates a diminished fifth. Because the top line is prominent throughout, no highlighting was added in this score.

Jean-Joseph Mouret (1682–1738) was one the most prominent composers of opera and instrumental music in France between Lully and Rameau. During this time, the splendor of Louis XIV (r. 1643–1715) and Louis XV (1715–1774) was unrivaled, as reflected in the palace of Versailles and in the grand entertainments at court. Like Lully, Mouret contributed numerous works to court celebrations, including several orchestral suites that were intended as grand *divertissements* (entertainments). The *Suite de symphonies* (1729) is scored for trumpets, oboes, bassoons, timpani and strings. The designation of specific instruments, along with their idiomatic treatment, is a significant step in the growth of the orchestral conception of instrumental music.

The *rondeau*, a French form that led to the later *rondo*, is in five parts: **A-B-A-C-A**. The **A** sections, consisting of antecedent and consequent melodic phrases, are in the tonic and feature the majestic sounds of trumpet and timpani. The contrasting sections project a quieter and gentler mood. The brief **B** section has a reduced texture of two voices, and the extended **C** section, set in parallel thirds, moves through several key areas, ending in A minor. This movement gained significant recognition in contemporary American life when it became the theme for *Masterpiece Theatre*, a popular PBS program since 1971.

29

Franz Joseph Haydn

String Quartet in D minor, Op. 76, No. 2 (*Quinten*),
Fourth movement (1797)

8CD: 2/ 57 – 62

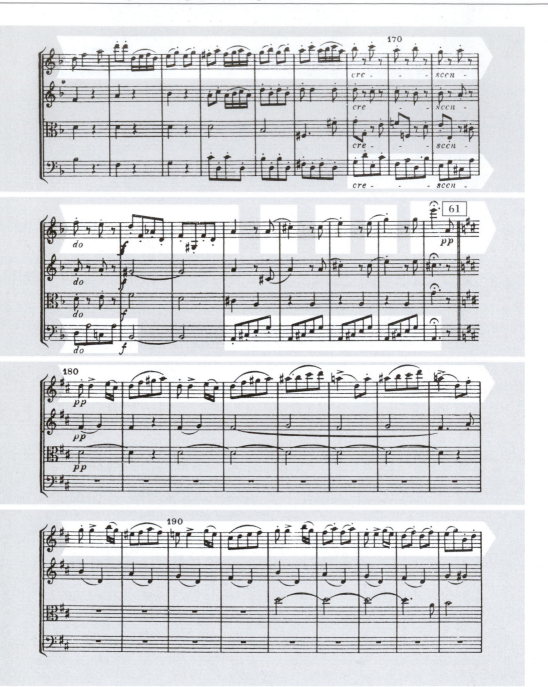

During the 1790s, the string quartet underwent a transformation from an intimate form of household entertainment to a theatrical concert piece. Elements of both conceptions can be seen in Haydn's late quartets. In the last movement of his String Quartet in D minor, Haydn mixes folk characteristics, virtuosic display, and humor within the framework of the sonata-allegro form. The exposition, written without repeats, presents three principal themes: the first is a binary tune suggesting a Hungarian dance, the second makes a brief appearance, and the closing theme appears over a tonic pedal. The development and recapitulation, in typical Haydn fashion, continue to delight with unexpected turns and flourishes. In the recapitulation, Haydn begins to develop ideas immediately at the close of the first theme, as he mixes various motives together. After a held dominant-seventh chord, the first theme returns quietly in D major, and this key remains through the recapitulation and the brief, theatrical coda.

30

Wolfgang Amadeus Mozart

Eine kleine Nachtmusik (A Little Night Music), K. 525
(1787)

8CD: 3/ 1 – 20
4CD: 1/ ⟨71⟩ – ⟨78⟩

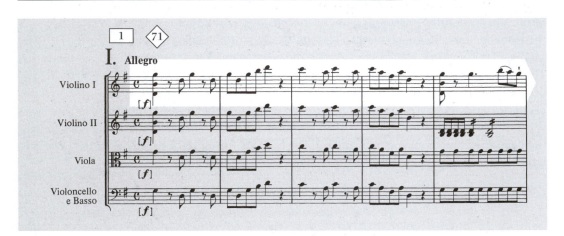

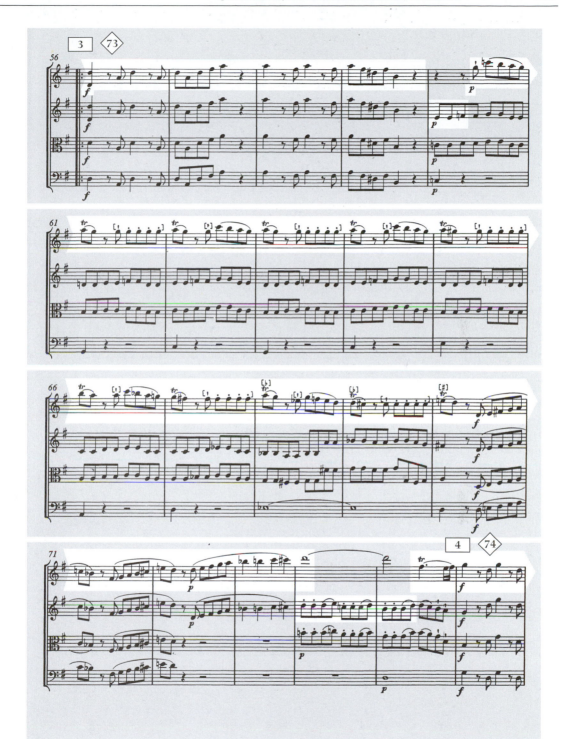

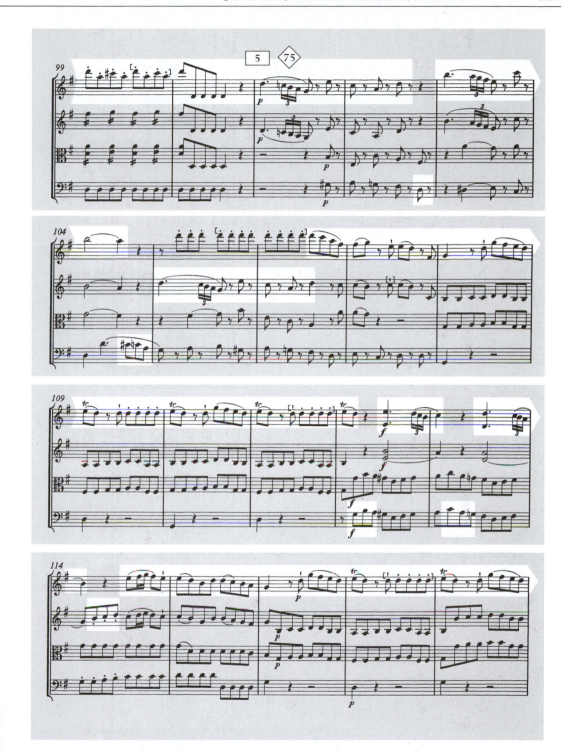

6

II. Romance

Andante

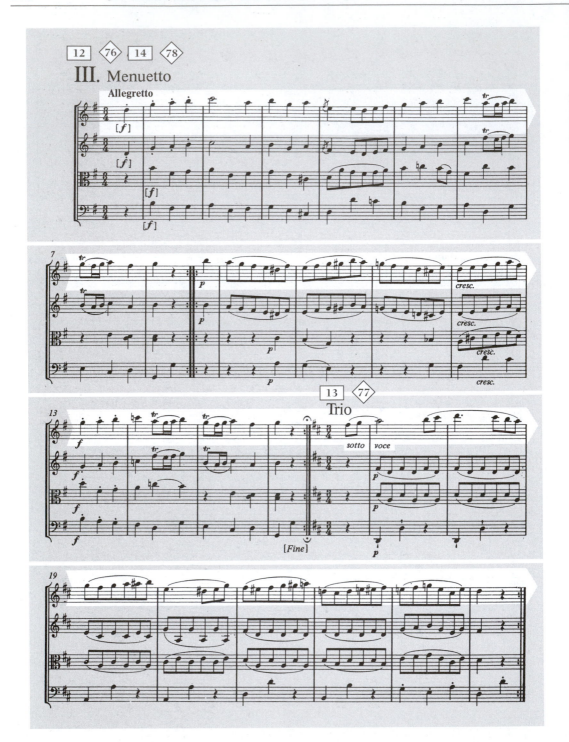

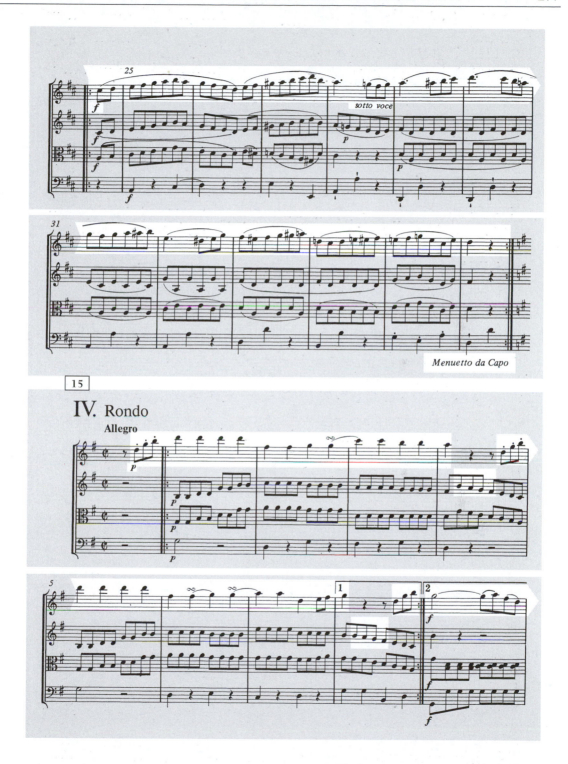

15

IV. Rondo

Allegro

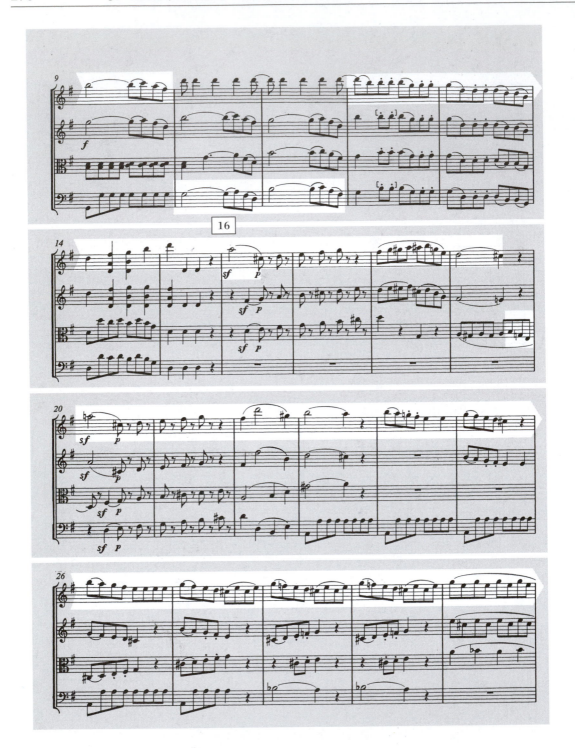

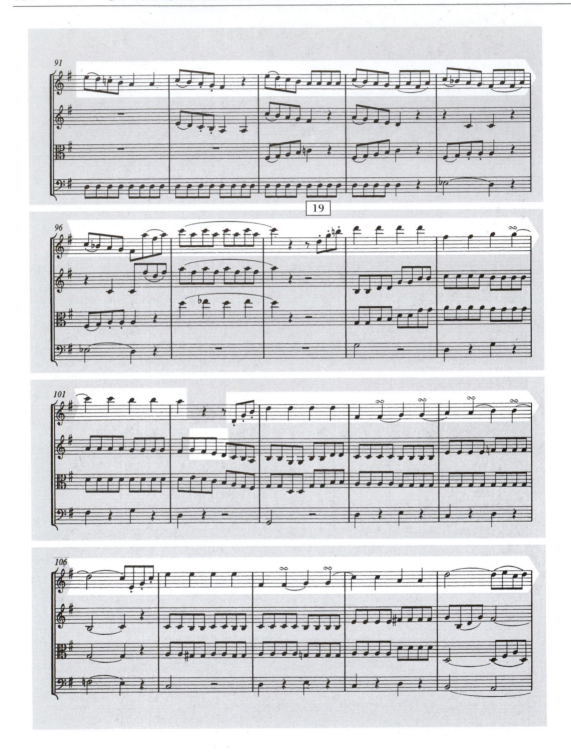

The instrumental serenade is a light entertainment work related to the divertimento. The term "serenade" suggests a nighttime performance, which is also reflected in the subtitle of Mozart's Serenade in D major, *Eine kleine Nachtmusik (A Little Night Music)*, although this title probably does not originate from Mozart. Like the divertimento, the serenade has no standard number of movements. *Eine kleine Nachtmusik* was originally created with five movements, but Mozart dropped one of the two minuets. As a result, the four remaining movements parallel the standard format of a symphony. While the nature of this work allows for a performance by a chamber ensemble, a chamber orchestral performance is Mozart's likely intention.

Although seemingly a simple work, *Eine kleine Nachtmusik* defines an important facet of Mozart's style with its tunefulness, elegance, and economical construction. The sonata-allegro first movement abounds with melodic motives. Three separate ideas are presented in the first theme alone, and both the second theme and closing theme provide strong contrasts. In a masterful stroke, all of the material of the exposition returns in the recapitulation essentially unaltered except for the subtle change in measure 99 that allows all of the remaining material to stay in the tonic. The development, which primarily focuses on the closing theme, and the coda are relatively brief and provide some harmonic contrast with chromatic inflections. In keeping with the tradition of binary structure, Mozart marks a repeat for the second half, which is sometimes observed in modern-day performances.

The middle movements are both set in clearly delineated forms. Typical of the instrumental Romanza, the second movement has a slow tempo, a lyrical principal theme, and a rondo structure. The minuet follows the standard structure. Most striking are the contrasts of moods between the vigorous opening, the elegant trio melody, and the subtle chromaticism near the end of the trio.

The delightful last movement deviates from standard classical forms. Labeled as a Rondo by Mozart, the Allegro can be seen as a hybrid structure with characteristics of both sonata-rondo and sonata-allegro forms. Regardless of the formal ambiguities, the lighthearted nature, flashy string techniques, and subtle references to motives from earlier movements make this a brilliant finale to the work as a whole.

31

Wolfgang Amadeus Mozart

Symphony No. 40 in G minor, K. 550, First movement
(1788)

8CD: 3/ 21 – 25

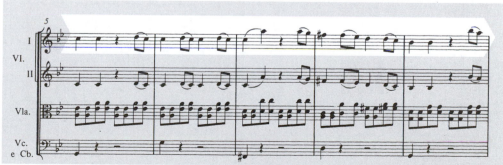

Editor's note: Square brackets indicate editorial additions.

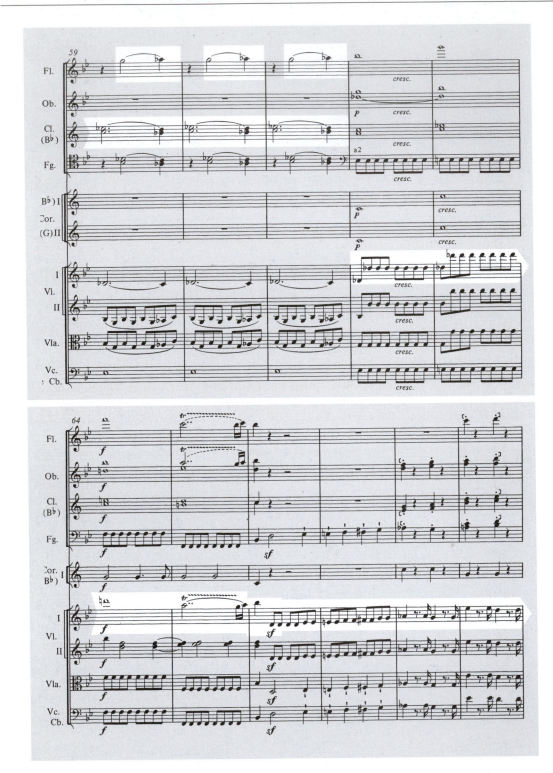

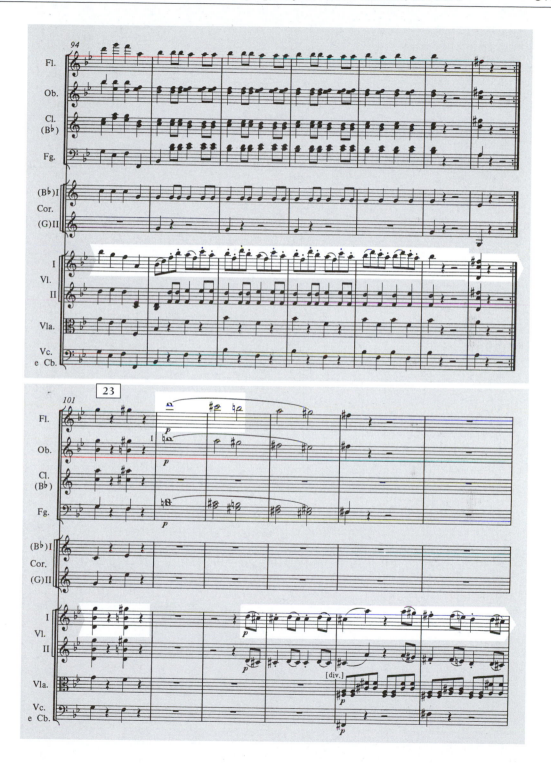

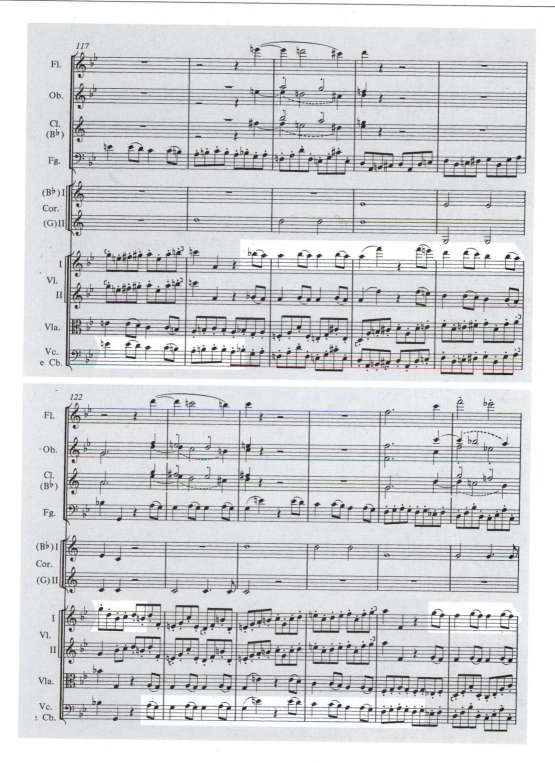

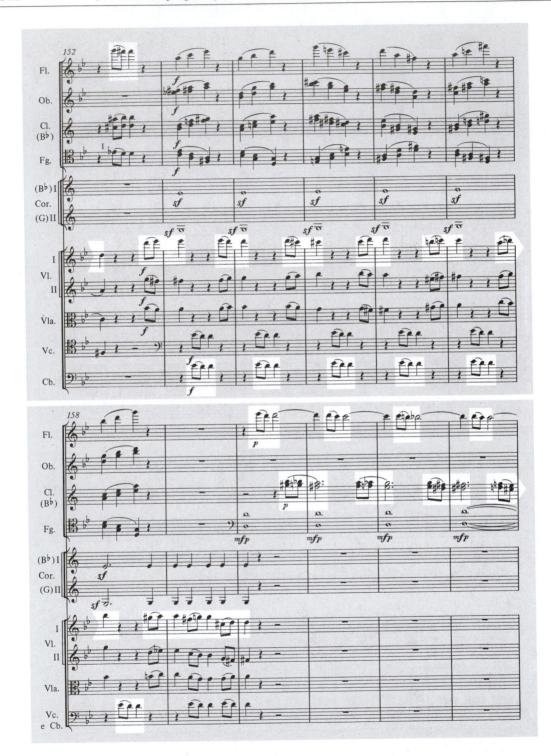

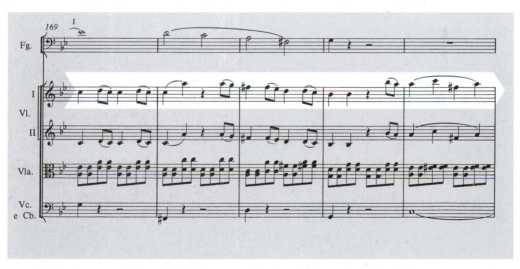

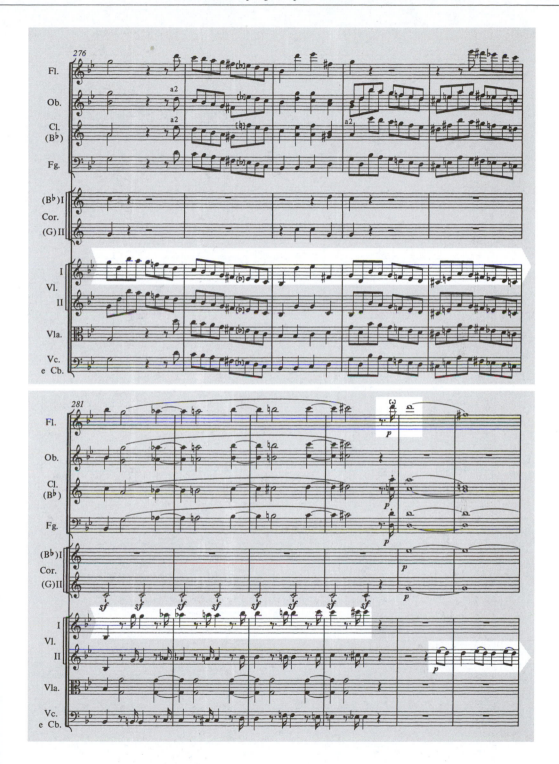

One of the most important developments of the Classical era was the emergence of the symphony. While three-movement works are not unusual in the genre at this time, the Viennese Classical style established a four-movement structure as the norm: sonata-allegro, slow movement, minuet, and fast finale. This format can be found in Mozart's last three symphonies (1788), which includes his darkest and most passionate work in the genre—the Symphony No. 40 in G minor.

Opening with a simple harmonic accompaniment, the first movement, in sonata-allegro form, presents a stark first theme built around a simple three-note motive. Both the rhythm of this motive and its reiterated half-step are important thematic ideas that are developed throughout the movement. The contrasting second theme appears in B-flat major, the relative major, during the exposition, but Mozart brings it back in G minor during the recapitulation, where its chromatic descents create a poignant mood. Unlike most minor-mode symphonies of the Classical era, Mozart maintains the minor key through its vigorous final cadence.

32

Franz Joseph Haydn

Symphony No. 94 in G major (*Surprise*),
Second movement (first performed 1792)

8CD: 3/ 26 – 32

4CD: 1/ 79 – 85

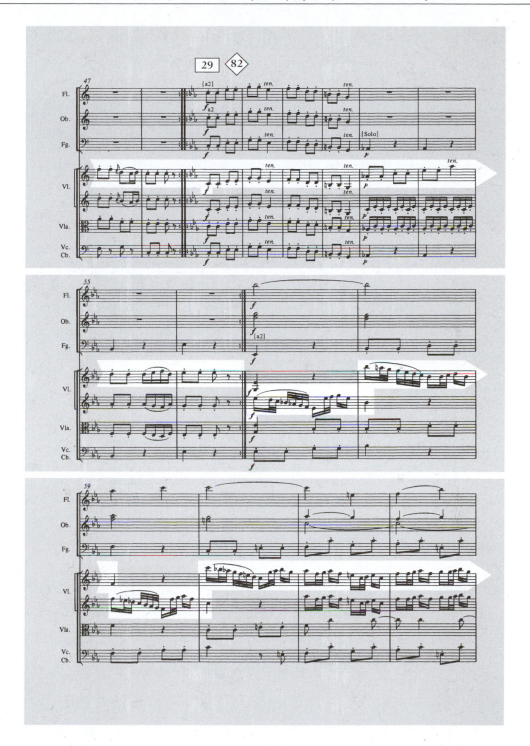

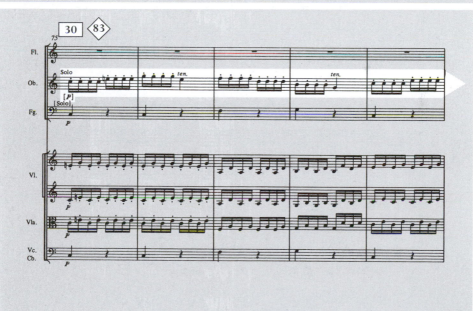

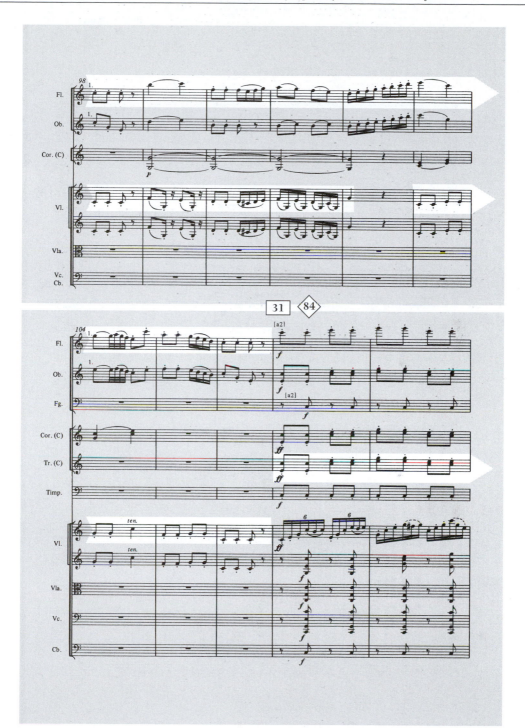

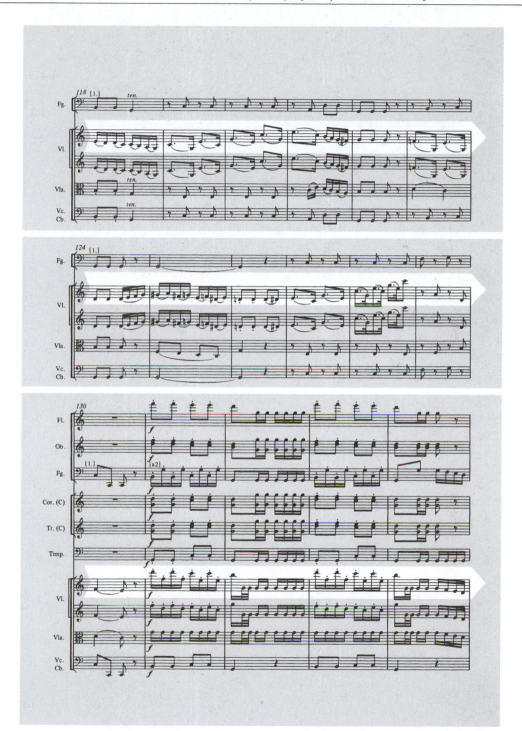

The last twelve symphonies of Franz Joseph Haydn (1732–1809) were written for subscription concerts in London directed by the violinist Johann Peter Salomon. Haydn himself played continuo on a fortepiano during the performances, while Salomon led the orchestra from the concertmaster position. The performance on period instruments in the accompanying recording allows us to hear the timbres and clarity of sound that would have delighted an eighteenth-century audience.

Haydn's Symphony No. 94 is clearly the most popular work of the *London Symphonies*. The work derives its nickname from the celebrated "surprise" that occurs in measure 16 of the second movement. The notoriety of this moment is well deserved, as it typifies Haydn's keen sense of wit and humor. The surprise is set up by the presentation of a quiet, simple melodic phrase, its repetition at an even softer dynamic level, and the placement of the jolt on the weak beat of the measure. The joke is made even more pronounced, as the orchestra continues to present the remainder of the rounded binary theme as if nothing had happened.

The simplicity of the theme-and-variations structure allows Haydn to play with the natural expectations of the listener. For the most part, the variations retain the tune and structure as heard in the opening theme. The most striking deviations occur in variations two and four. The second variation, which begins with two sudden harmonic shifts to C minor and E-flat major, launches into an intense developmental passage that replaces the second half of the theme. Variation four presents variations within a variation, as the repetition of each phrase is altered. A coda follows that features fleeting fragments of the tune in the winds, over chromatic harmonies in the strings.

33

Ludwig van Beethoven

Symphony No. 5 in C minor, Op. 67 (1807–8)

8CD: 3/ 33 – 57
4CD: 2/ 4 – 28

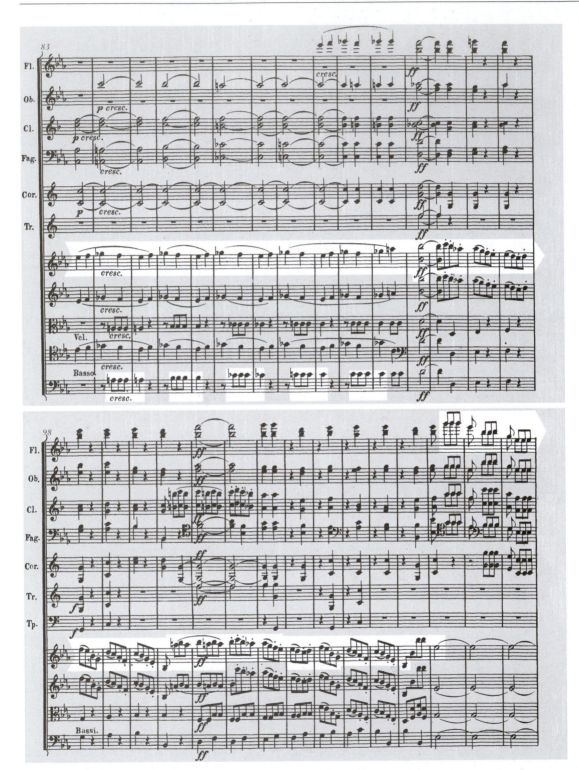

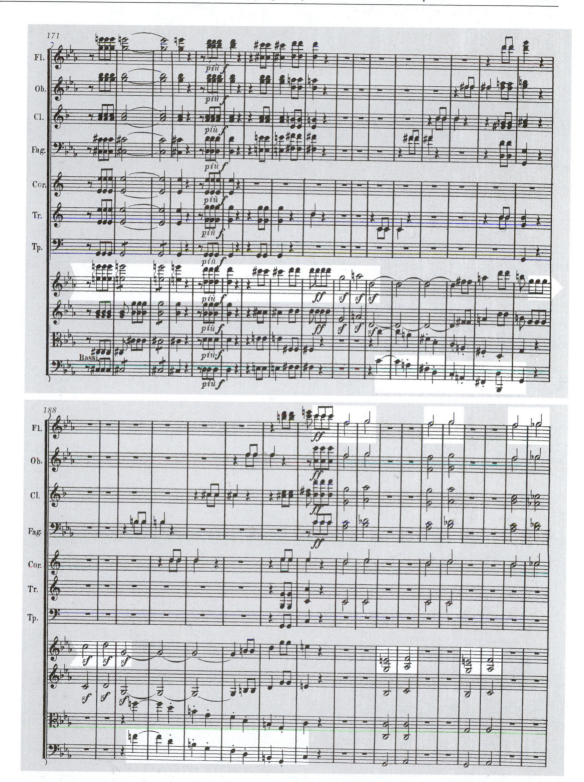

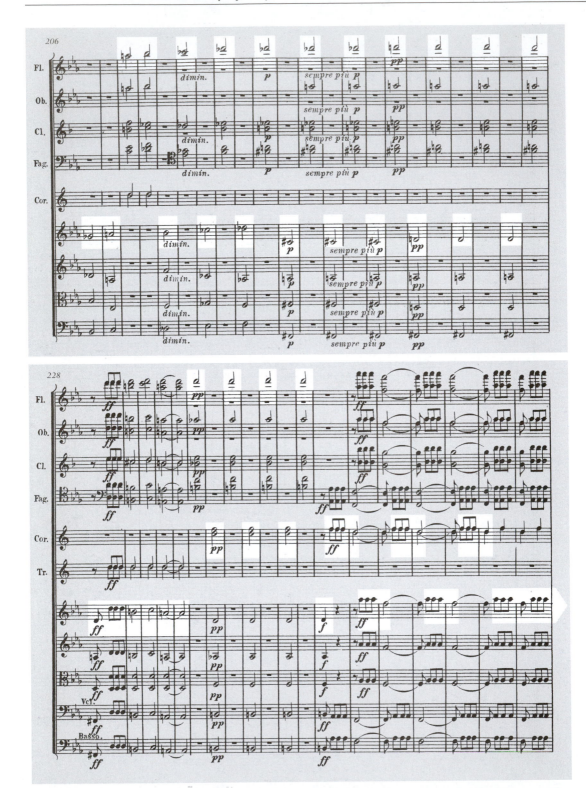

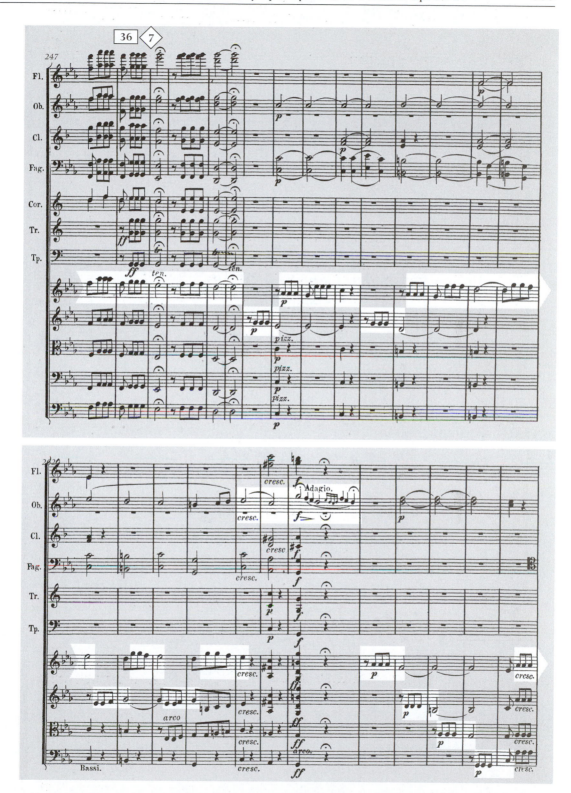

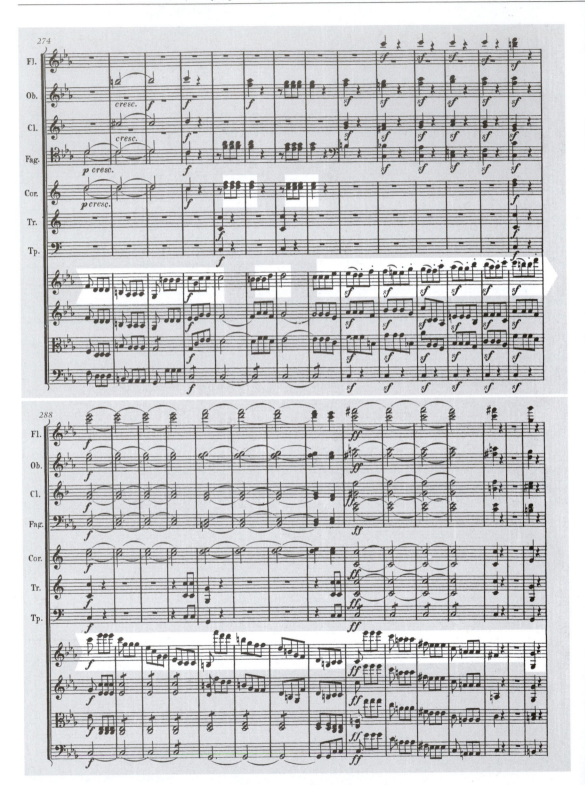

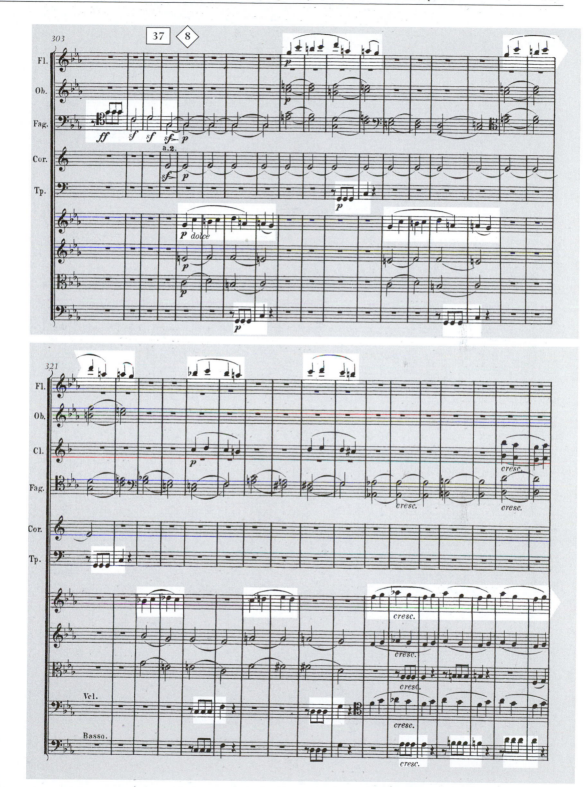

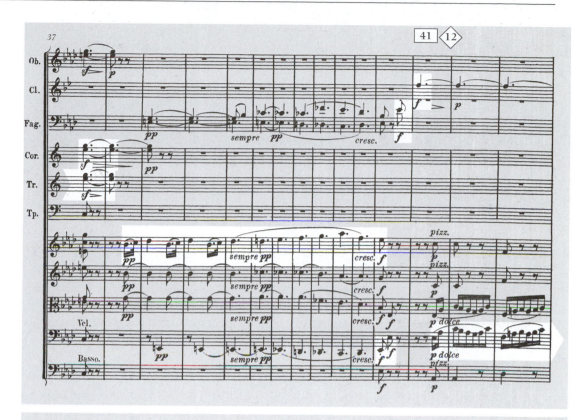

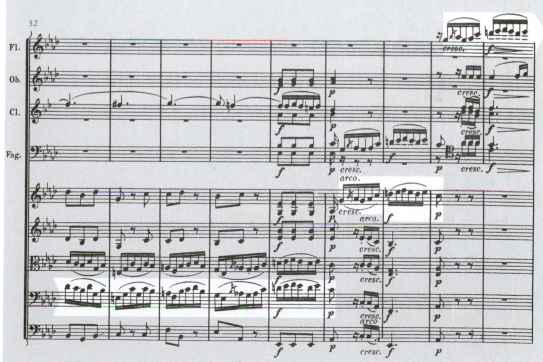

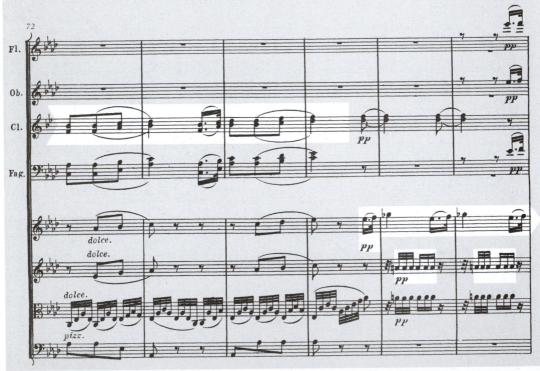

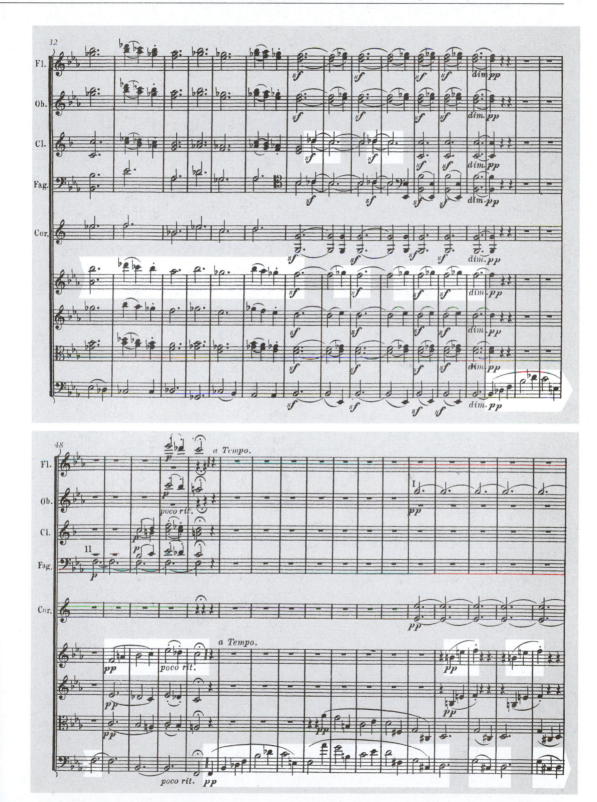

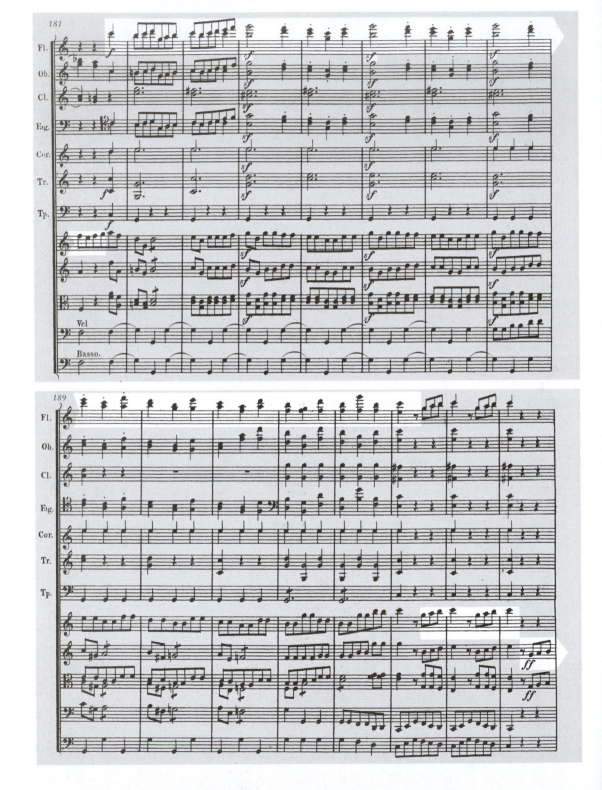

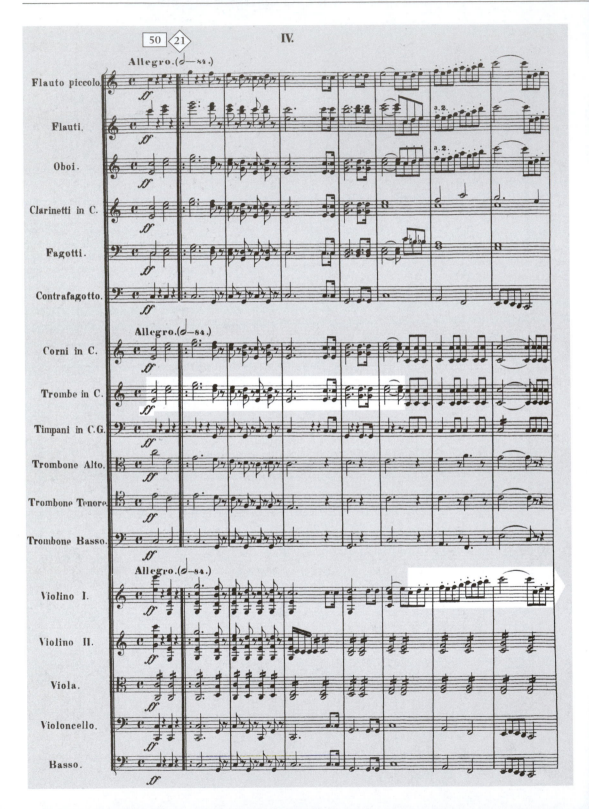

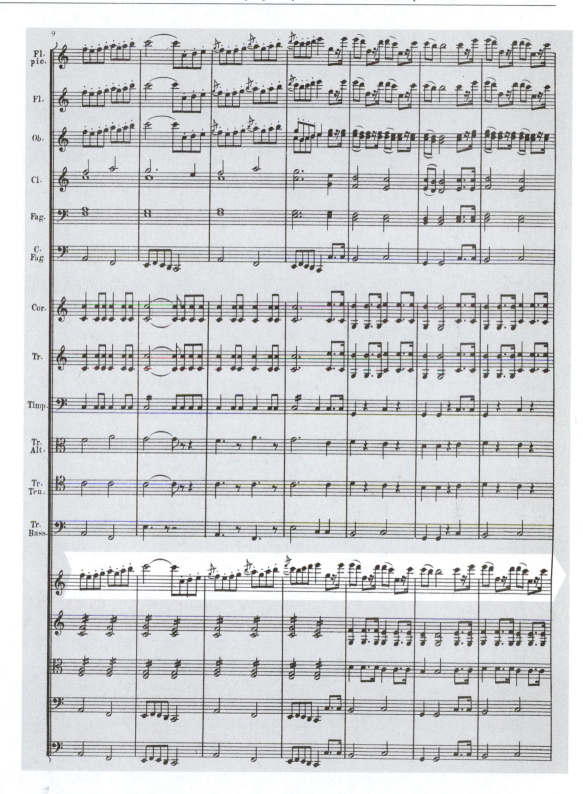

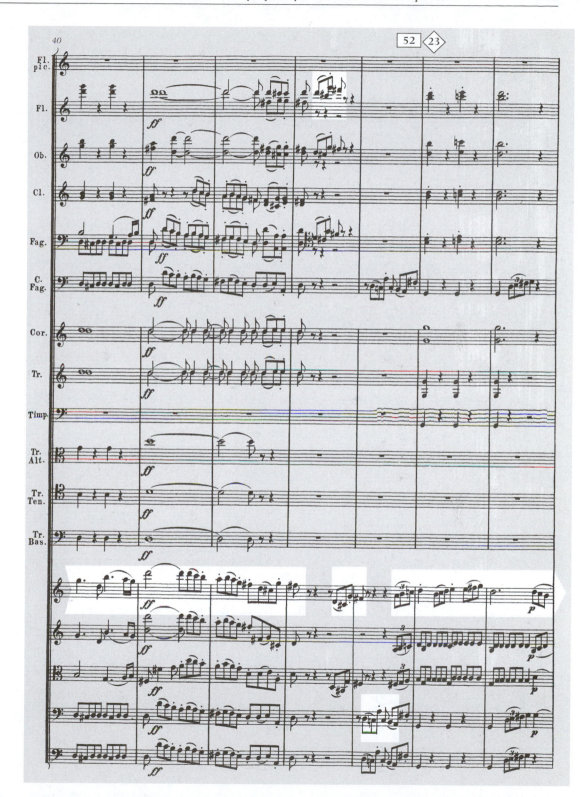

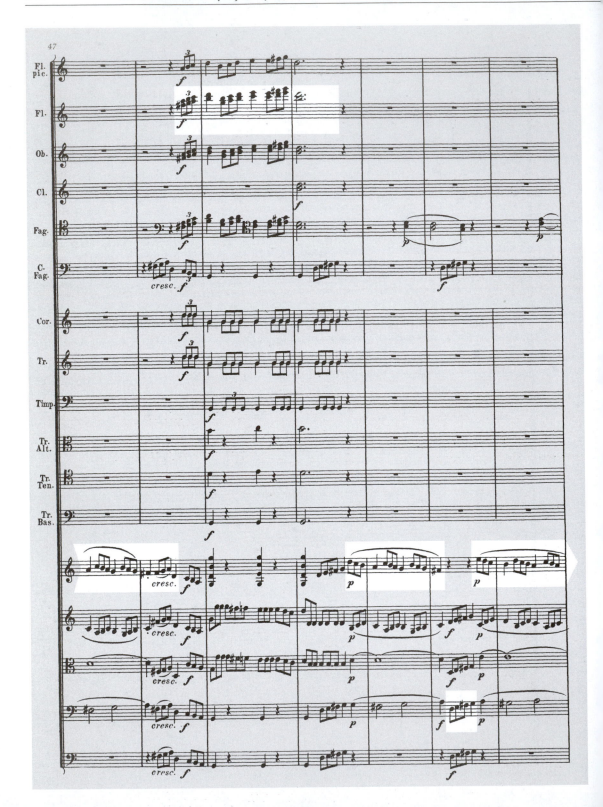

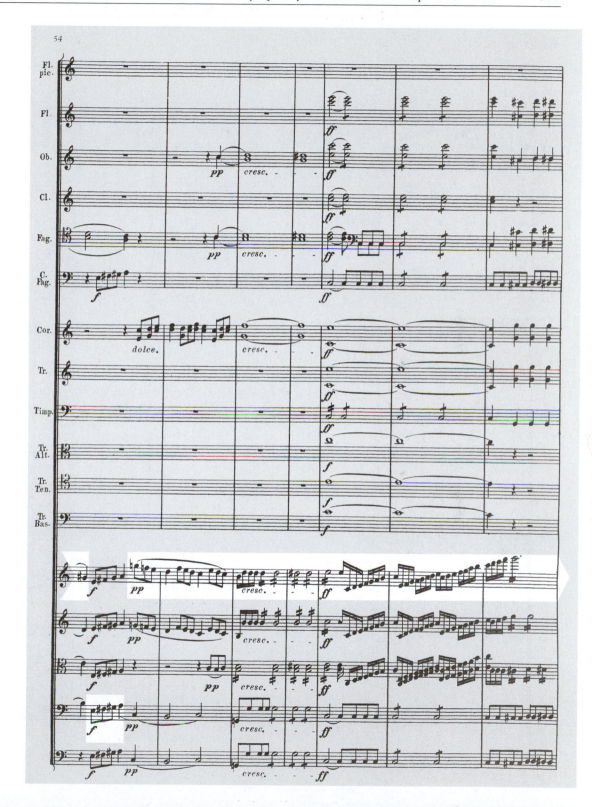

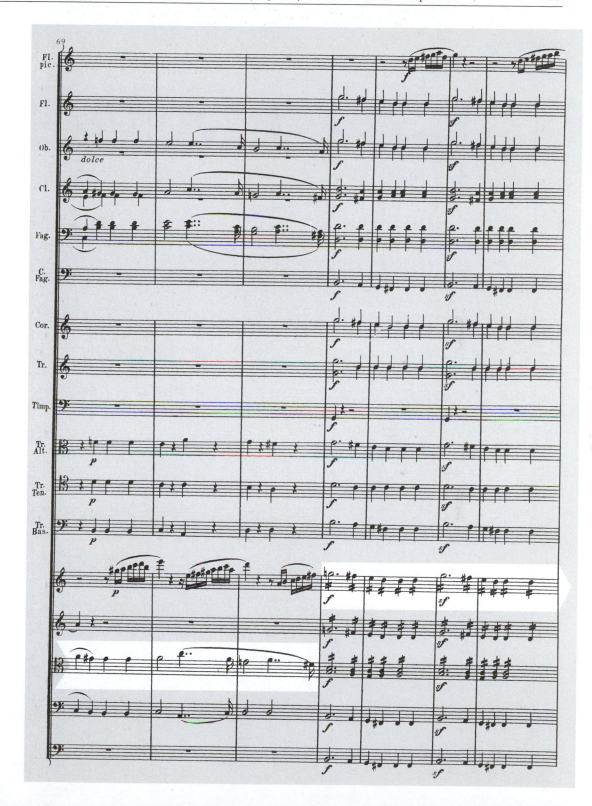

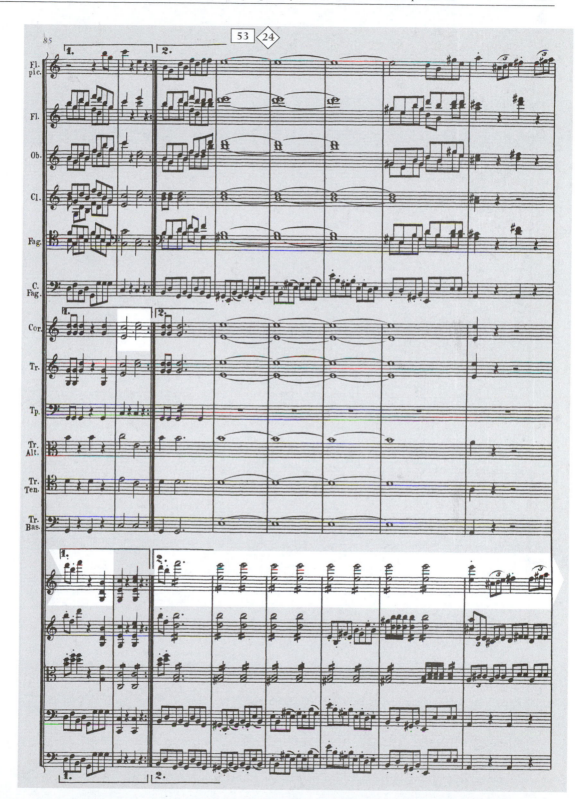

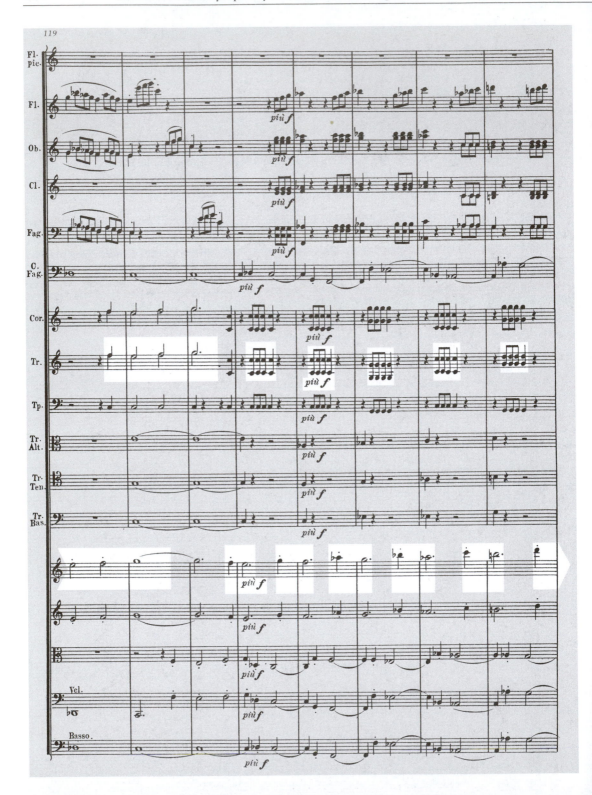

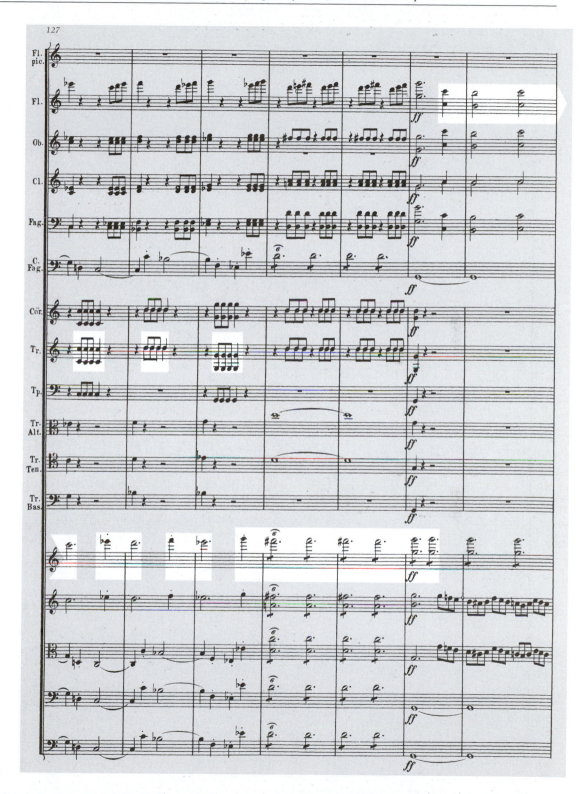

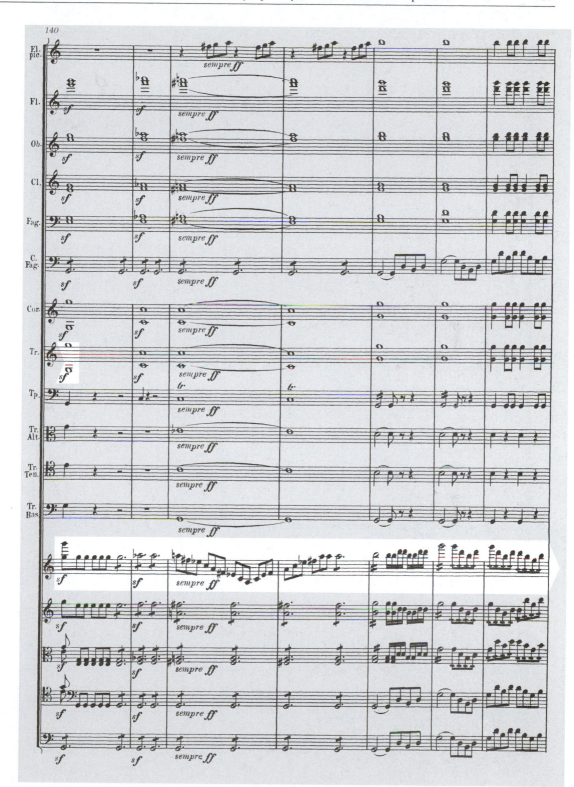

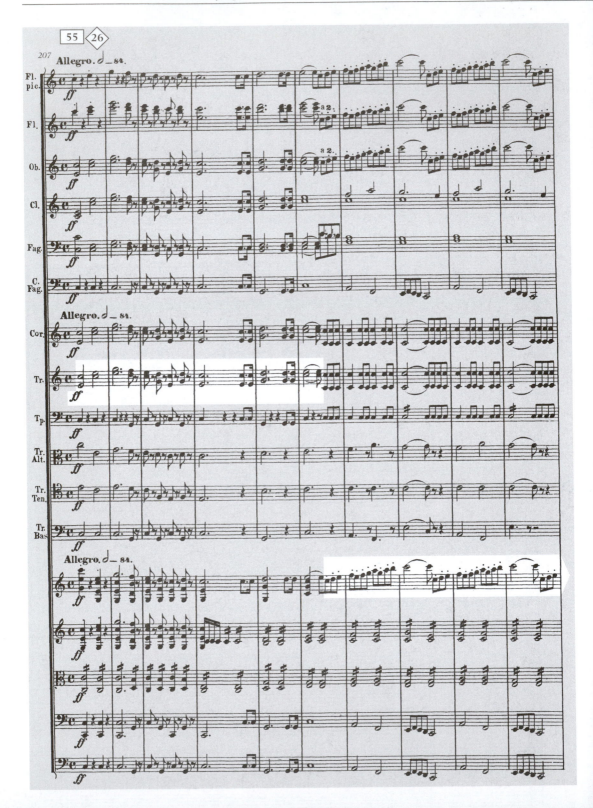

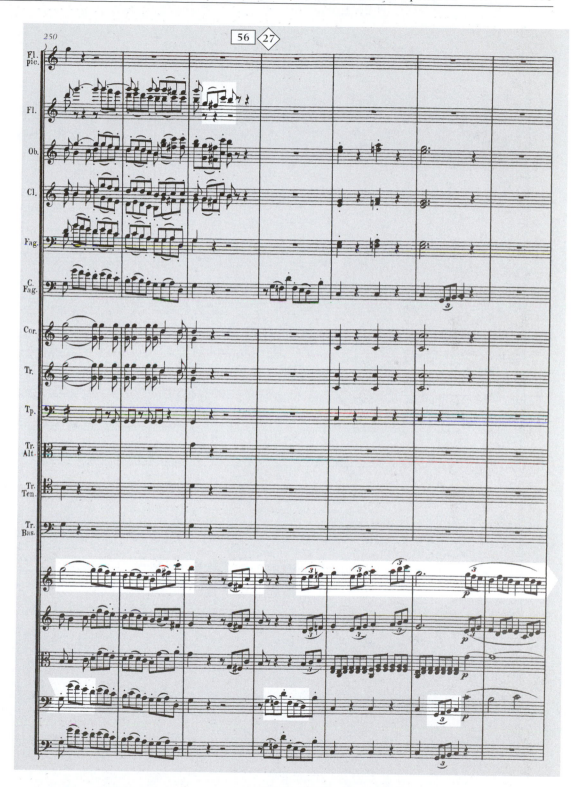

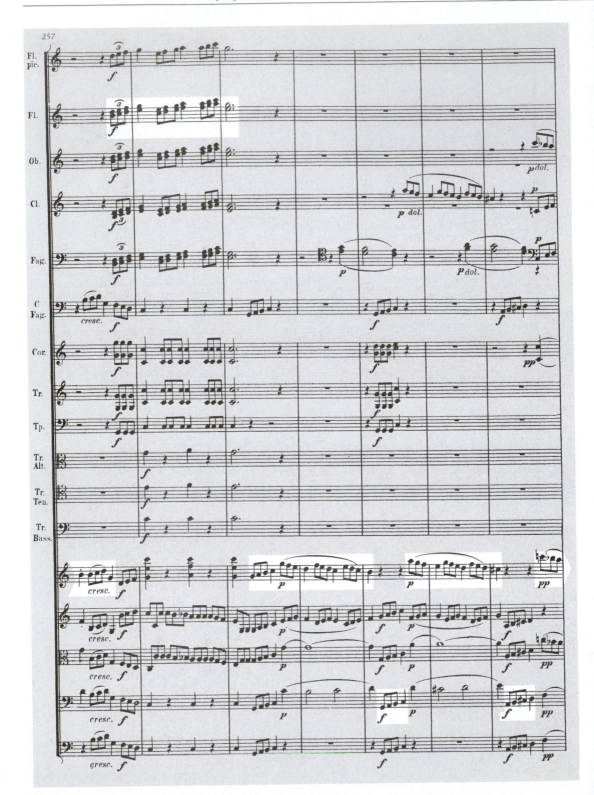

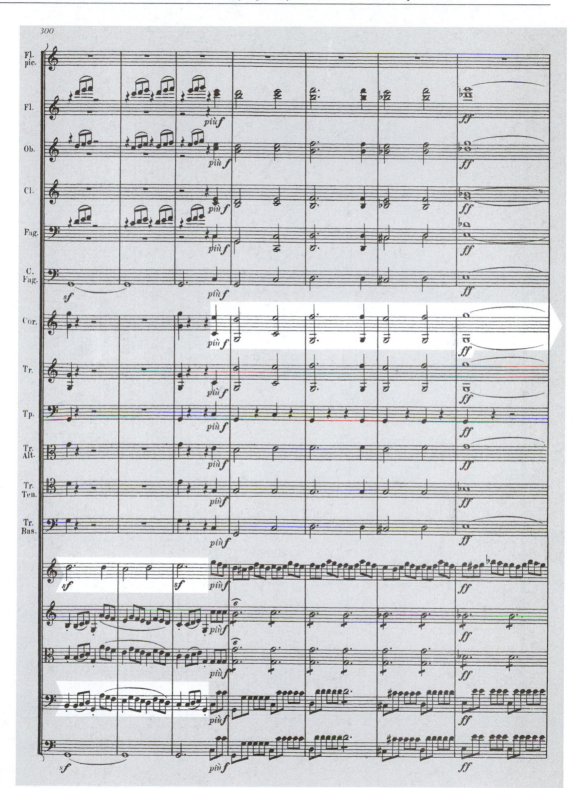

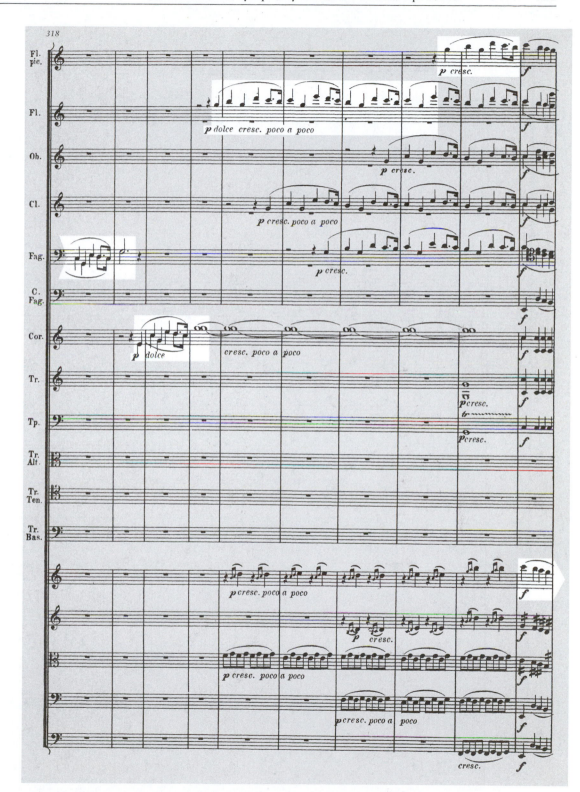

328

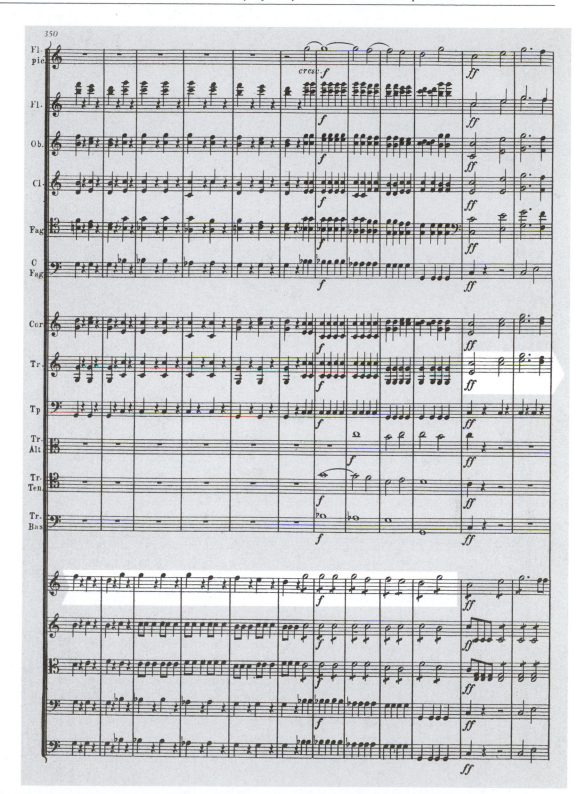

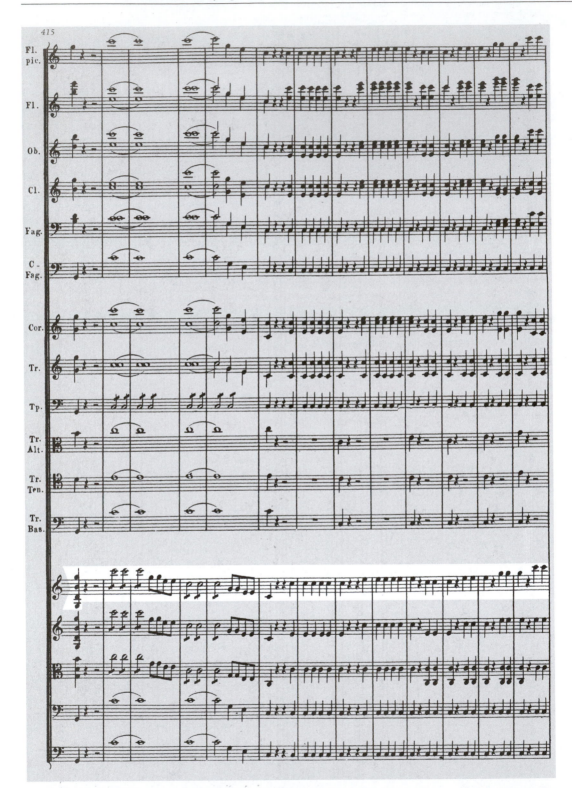

Beethoven's landmark symphony provides a model for concise, dramatic, and unified musical expression. In this work, Beethoven establishes the basic techniques of creating cyclic unity. Rather than treating each movement in the symphony as a separate entity, as in earlier works of the genre, Beethoven links them together with a common motive, a transition between the third and fourth movements, and a quotation of the third movement prior to the recapitulation in the fourth movement.

The four-note motive sounded at the outset of the symphony can be heard in all four movements. It is the principal motive of the sonata-allegro first movement. The radiant second movement, a loose theme-and-variations structure, features two thematic ideas. The rhythmic motive can most readily be heard in the second idea, especially on its repetition where it is emphasized by the brass and timpani. Although the third movement maintains the basic ternary **A-B-A** structure, triple meter, and quick tempo associated with a scherzo, the treatment of the material is unusual. The opening scherzo abandons the expected binary form for a simple alternation of two ideas: a mysterious theme in the lower strings and a forceful statement of the principal rhythmic motive in the horns. Surprisingly, the return of the scherzo brings a complete change of character, as Beethoven quietly leads us into a transition.

The dramatic crescendo into the finale ushers in a triumphant theme. Adding to the weight of this moment is the first appearance of the piccolo, contrabassoon, and trombones. Such power and force for a finale is unprecedented. Previously, the weight of the symphony had been on the first movement, and the last movement was generally light hearted. The second theme of the sonata-allegro structure features repeated statements of the four-note motive in diminution over a simple accompaniment motive. In the development, this accompaniment emerges as a powerful force and propels the movement into a quotation of the third movement, a repeat of the transition, and an exultant arrival at the recapitulation.

34

Wolfgang Amadeus Mozart

Piano Concerto in G major, K. 453 (1784)

Editor's note: The cadenzas included in this score are Mozart's own.

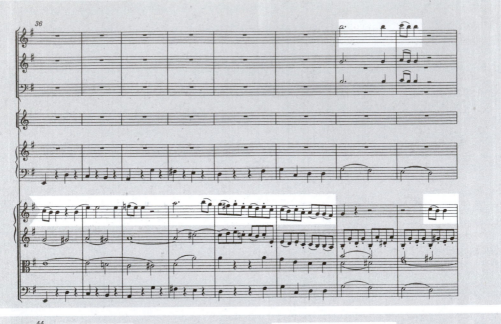

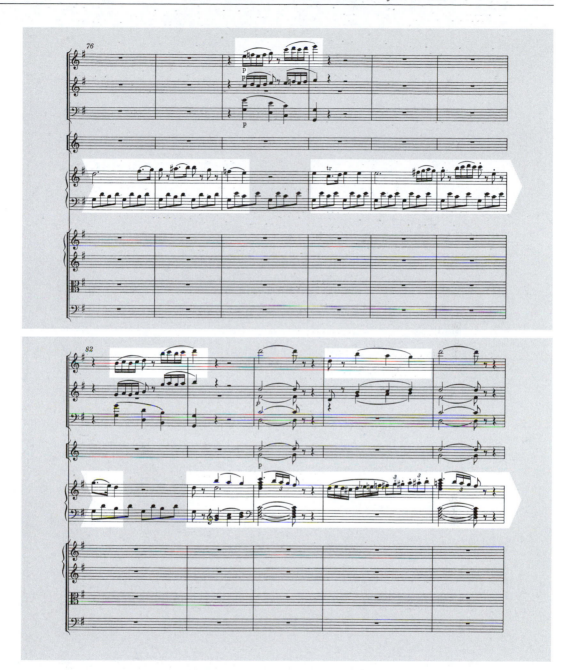

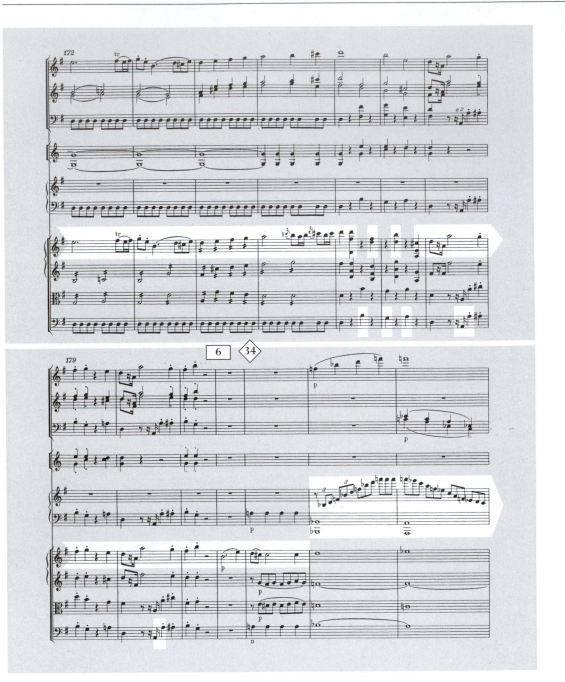

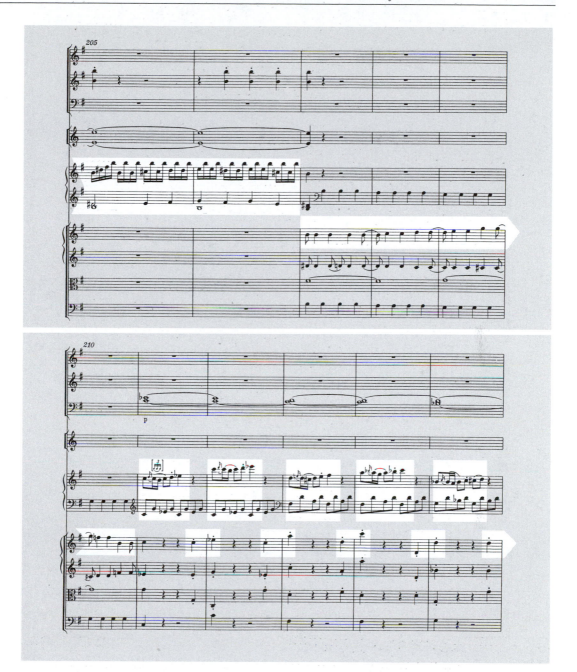

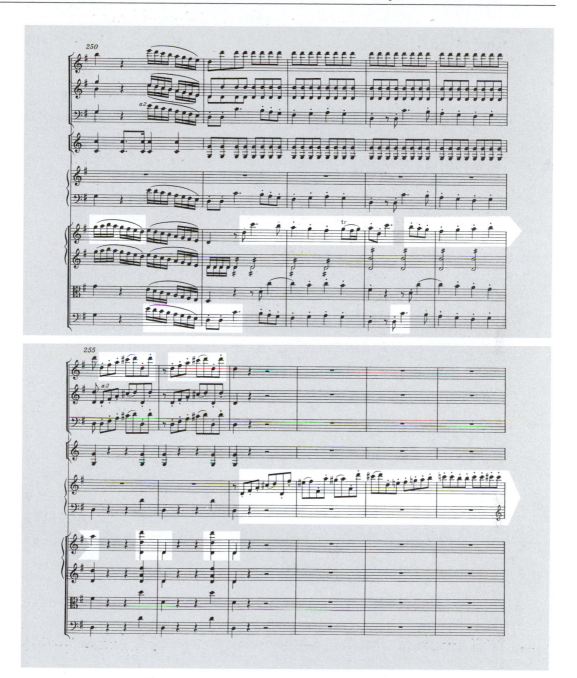

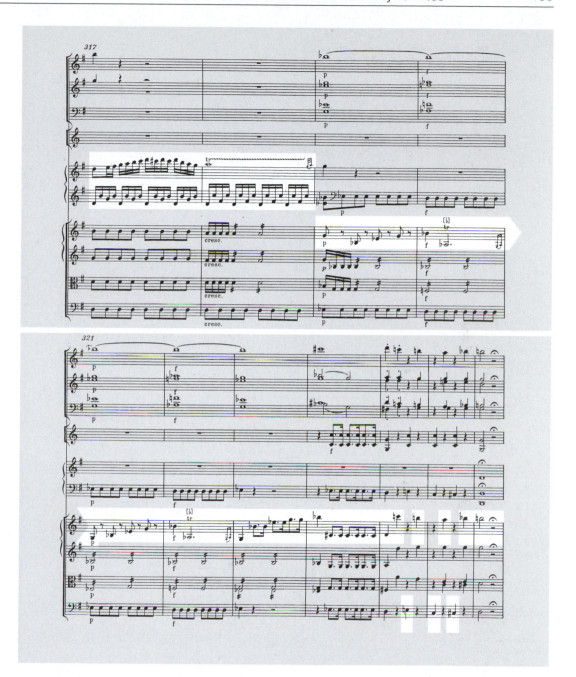

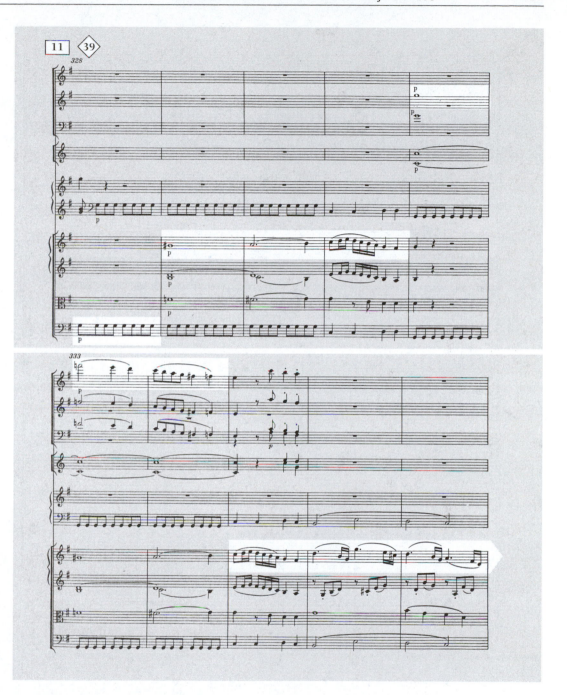

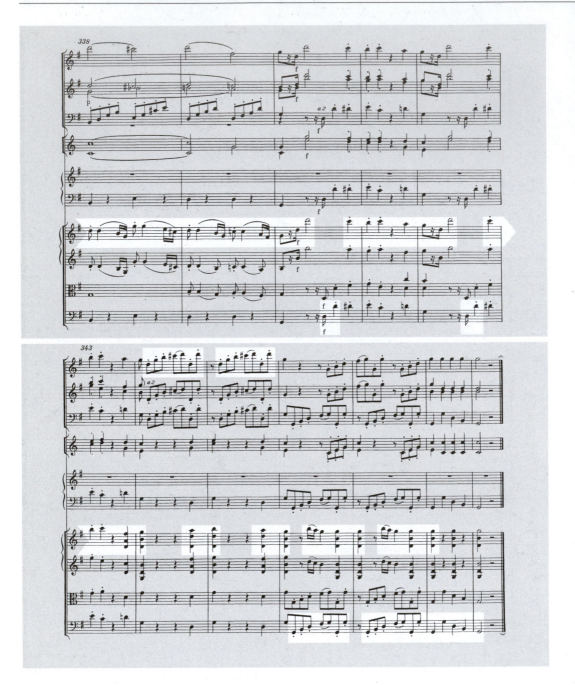

II

Andante

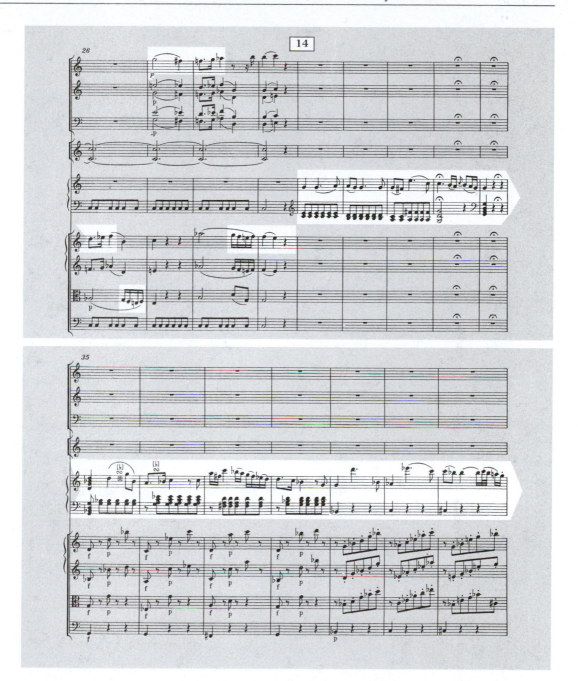

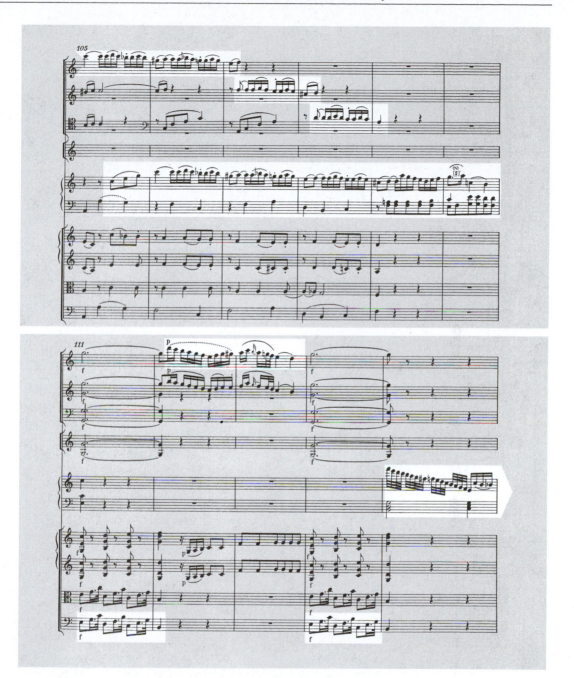

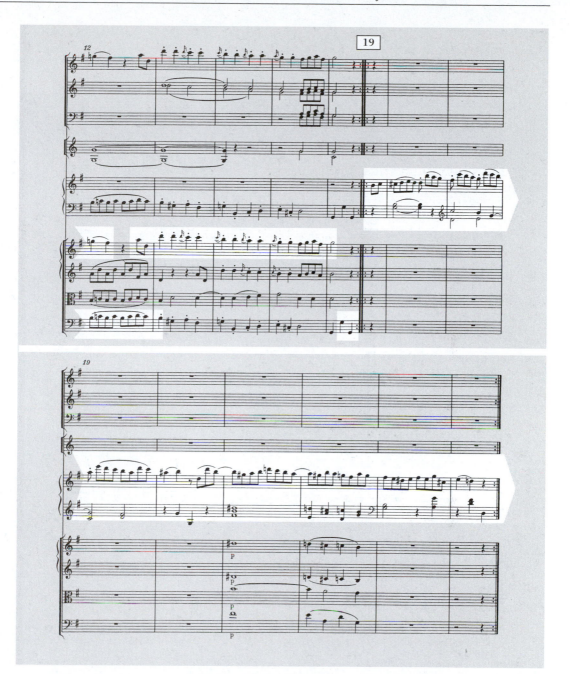

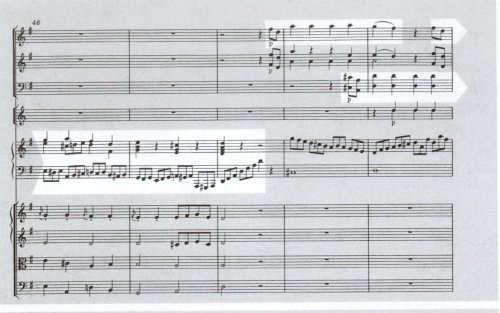

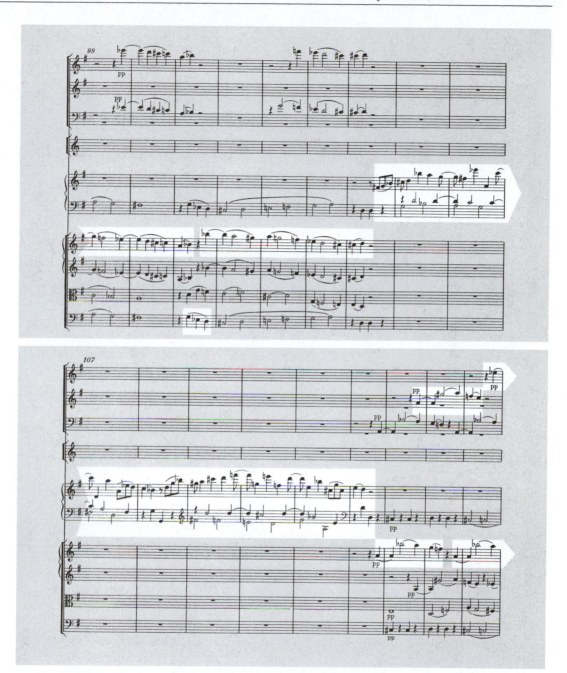

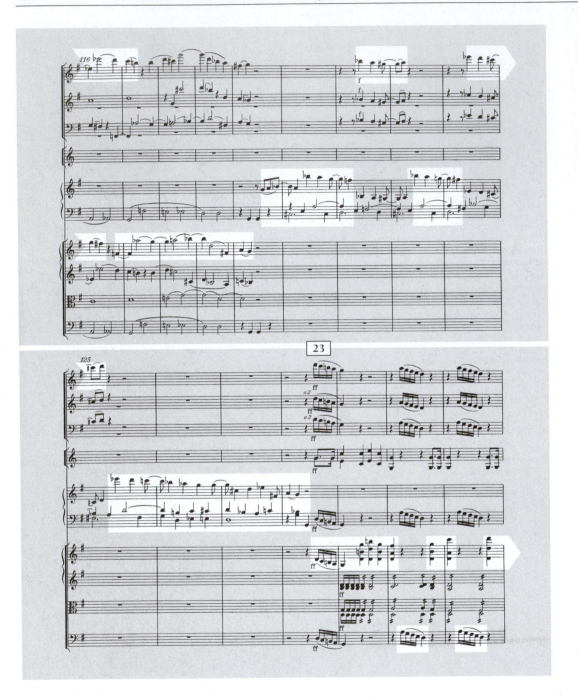

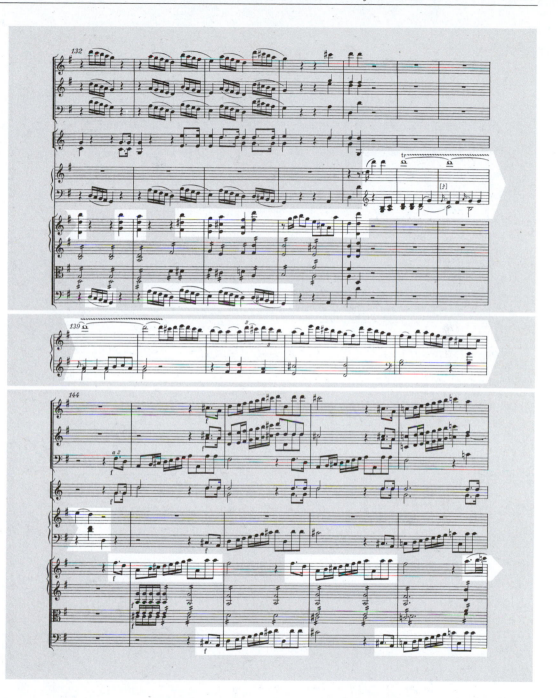

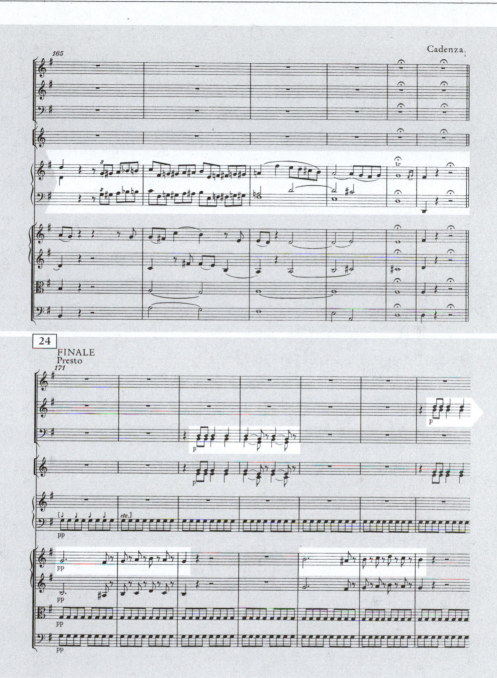

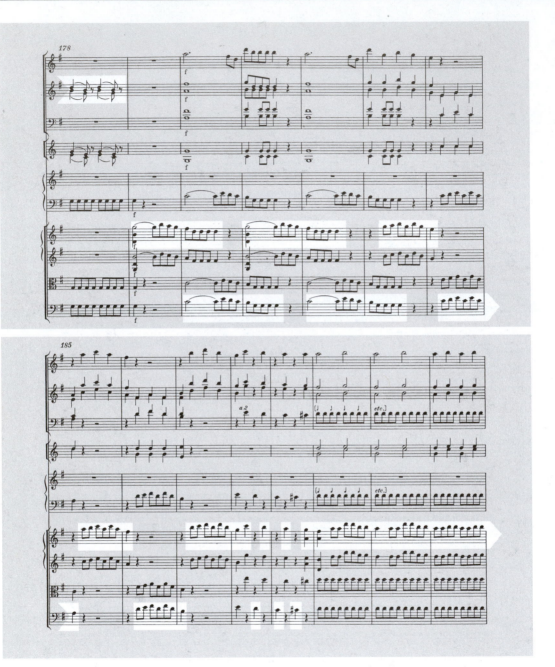

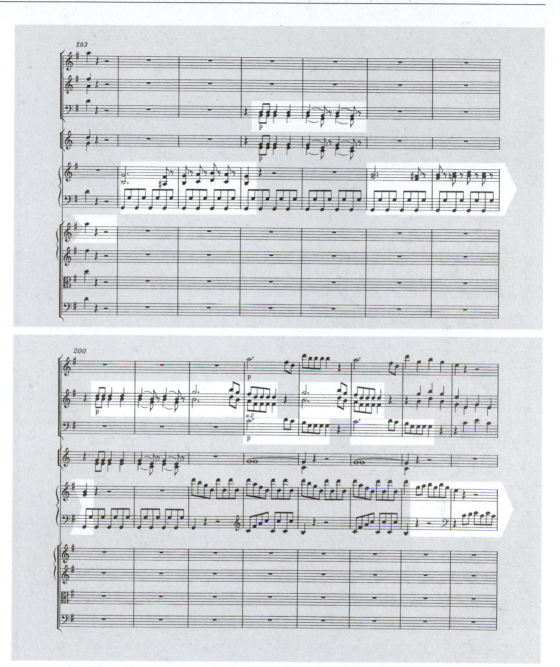

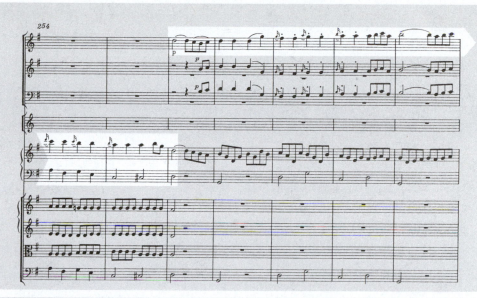

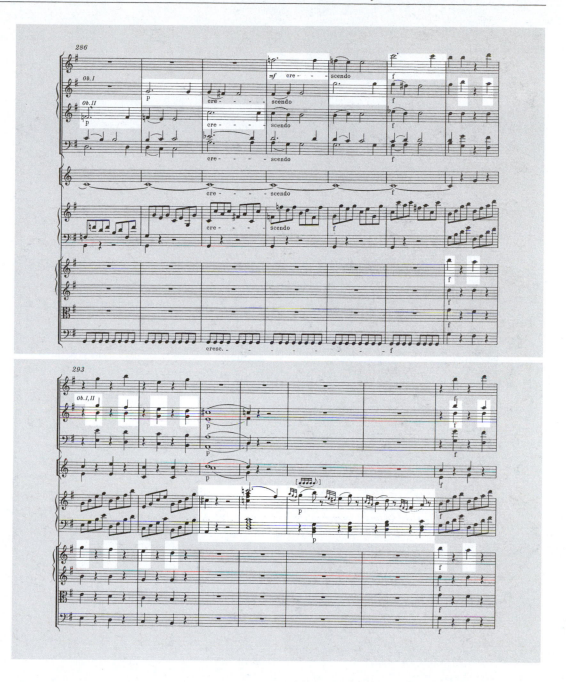

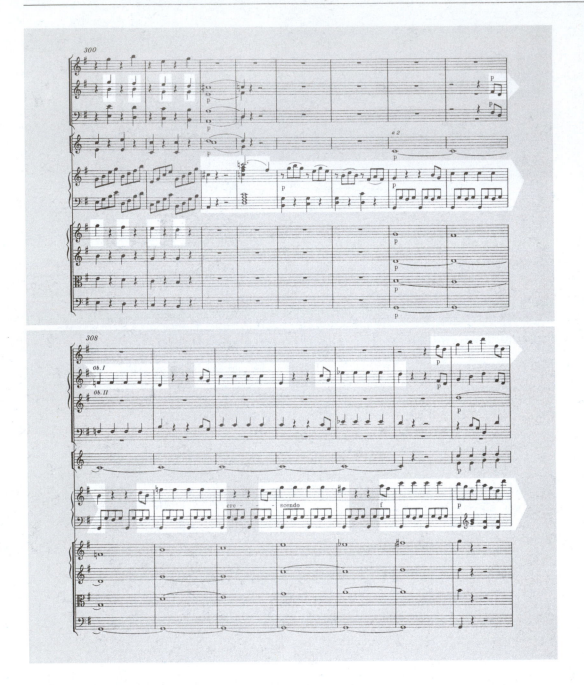

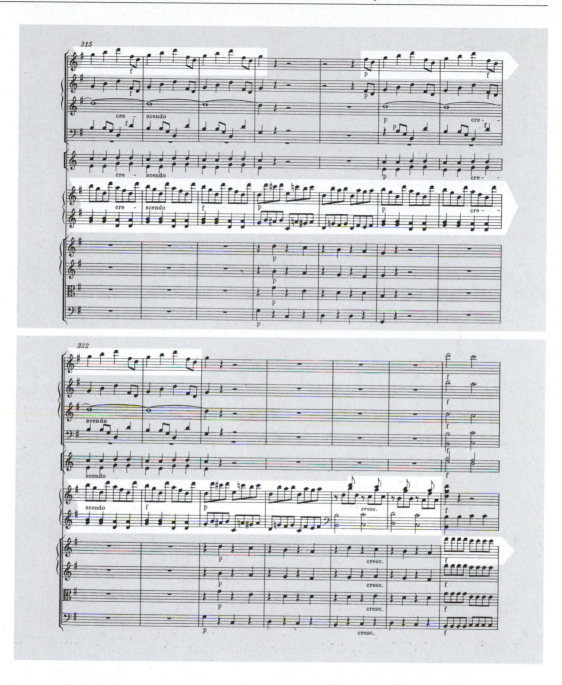

Mozart plays a critical role in the history of the piano concerto. Generally written for his own performance, Mozart's concertos mix the elegance of his own natural style with the virtuosic display and dramatic flair of Classical-era concert music. His most important formal contribution in the genre is the fusion of the Baroque ritornello procedures with the principles of Classical sonata-allegro form.

In the Piano Concerto in G major, K. 453, Baroque influences can be seen in its three-movement structure and in the alternation of *tutti* and solo sections. Within this Baroque framework, Mozart introduces elements of sonata-allegro form, including contrasting expositions by the *tutti* orchestra and solo piano, a development, and a recapitulation. The movement closes with a final *tutti* section that contains a cadenza composed by Mozart.

The form of the slow movement is similar to that of the first movement. The *tutti* begins with a haunting five-measure theme followed by a number of other thematic ideas. The pianist repeats the opening five-measure theme, but uses its harmonic ambiguity to begin moving to the dominant key. The first theme continues to mark important arrival points throughout the movement: it functions as a transition from the exposition to the development, it initiates the recapitulation, and, in an altered form, it signals the end of the movement.

The theme-and-variations final movement follows a typical scenario. The theme is a lighthearted rounded binary tune. The first two variations maintain the repeats of the original theme, while the final three variations have written-out repeats, alternating material between orchestra and soloist. The fourth variation is in the obligatory minor key, and the fifth provides a vigorous climax. The movement closes with an exuberant free fantasy that incorporates material from the principal theme.

35

Franz Joseph Haydn

Trumpet Concerto in E-flat major, Third movement
(1796)

8CD: 4/ 25 – 30

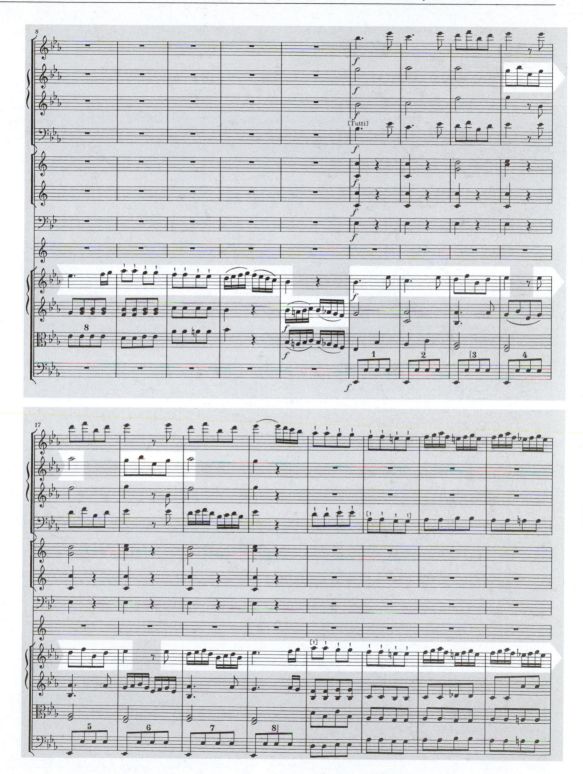

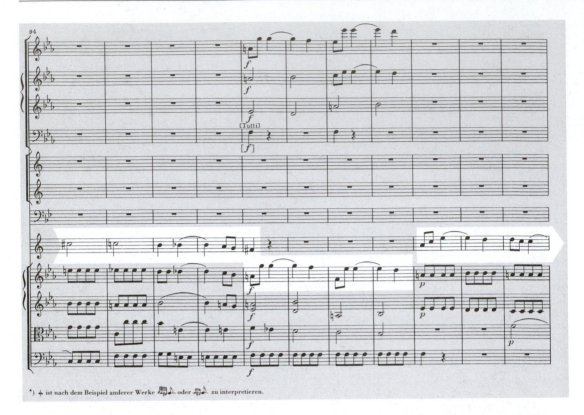

*) ♩ ist nach dem Beispiel anderer Werke 🎵♪ oder 🎵♪ zu interpretieren.

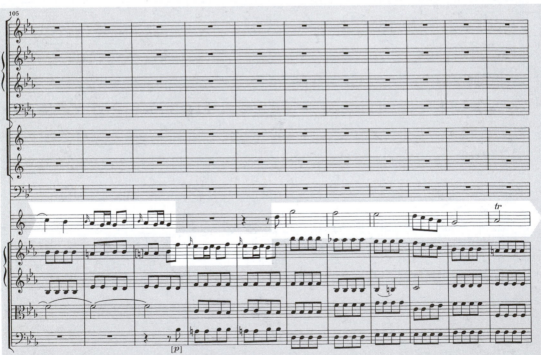

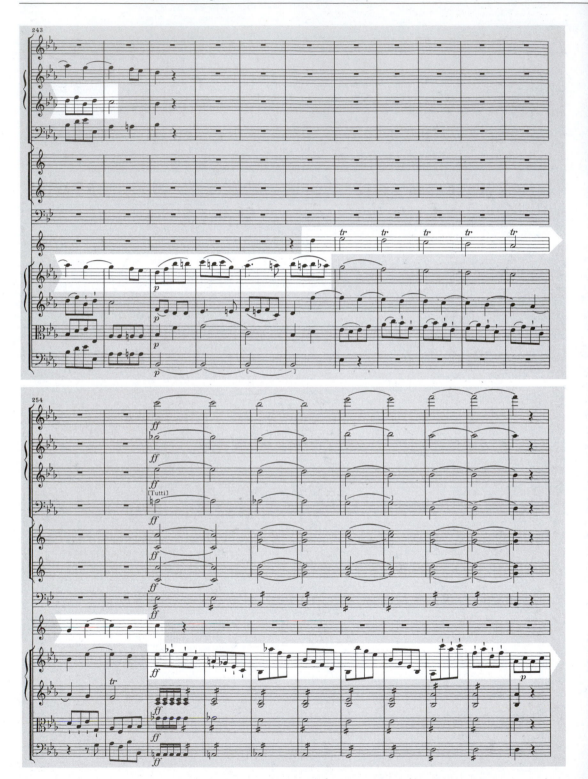

Haydn's prolific output includes over thirty concertos for various solo instruments. The Trumpet Concerto in E-flat major, completed in 1796, is Haydn's last work for orchestra. Set in the standard three-movement structure, the concerto exhibits a masterful blend of Baroque and Classical forms and idiomatic writing for the solo trumpet.

The final movement combines Baroque ritornello structure with Classical sonata-rando form, resulting in an **A-B-A-B-A-C-A-B-A** pattern. As in the Baroque ritornello form, the orchestra opens with the two principal themes (mm. 1 and 27) in the tonic. The trumpet soloist repeats the orchestral material, with the **B** theme given in the dominant (m. 80). Following the return of **A**, section **C** serves as a development section, complete with modulations and imitation. The recapitulation begins in m. 181, and theme **B** remains firmly in the tonic.

The triadic and disjuct nature of the thematic material is well suited to the trumpet, and passages of scales, arpeggios, and trills create several moments of virtuosic display. Typical of Haydn are the frequent dialogues between soloist and orchestra and the underlying humor created by abrupt dynamic changes, surprise harmonies, and unexpected rests.

36

Wolfgang Amadeus Mozart

Piano Sonata in A major, K. 331, Third movement (1783)

The piano sonata became one of the most popular genres of the Classical era. Although the number of movements varies from two to four, the individual movements of a sonata approximate the form and style of their counterparts in a symphony. The rondo finale to the three-movement Piano Sonata in A major, K. 331, by W. A. Mozart (1756–1791), is set in an unusual format: **A-B-C-B-A-B-coda**. The performance with a fortepiano on the recording brings out the different timbres of the registers and provides great clarity both to the sixteenth note passages and to individual chords.

At the time that this sonata was composed (1783), Vienna was under the spell of the exotic styles and sounds of Turkey. Mozart exploited this fascination with Turkey throughout the movement. The clanging sounds of a Turkish Janissary band can be heard in Mozart's rolled chords, quick ornaments, and drones. Another fascinating Turkish tradition is the whirling dervish ritual, a dance featuring a controlled spinning motion, which is suggested by the continuous whirling sixteenth-note material of sections **A** and **C**.

37

Ludwig van Beethoven

Piano Sonata No. 14 in C-sharp minor, Op. 27, No. 2
(*Moonlight*) (1801)

8CD: 4/ 38 – 51
4CD: 2/ ◇40◇ – ◇48◇

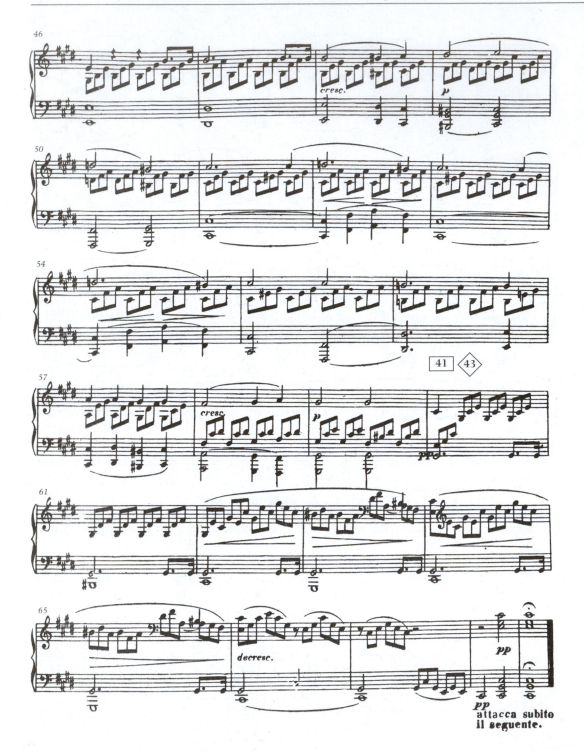

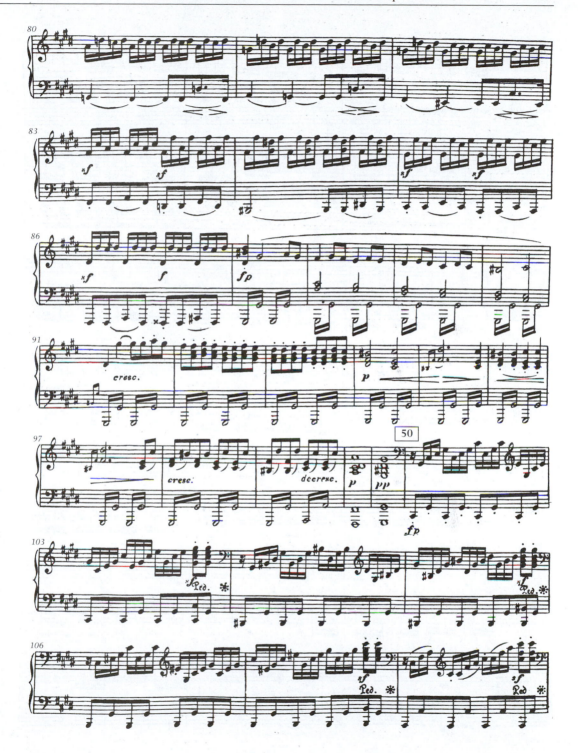

Beethoven came to Vienna in 1792 and quickly established himself as a virtuoso pianist and composer. For nearly a decade, Beethoven's principal compositions were piano sonatas. Among his most popular sonatas from this period is Op. 27, No. 2 (1801), which was given the subtitle "Moonlight" after the composer's death.

Beethoven called the work a *Sonata quasi una Fantasia* (a fantasy sonata), and several qualities of a fantasy can be observed. Most striking is the celebrated opening movement. Instead of the standard sonata-allegro, Beethoven begins with an *Adagio sostenuto*. The unrelenting eighth-note motion in a compound meter, the dark key of C-sharp minor, and the continually shifting harmonies create an expressive, dreamlike state. The haunting mood of the movement can also be attributed to its songlike quality. The first four measures establish an accompaniment pattern, and the melodic entrance with repeated pitches suggests the singing of words. The overall form is similar to the modified strophic song form that would be used extensively in the nineteenth century. Sonata-form principles can still be detected in the movement, as the poignant melodic phrase beginning in measure 15, set in B major (the dominant of the relative major E) returns in the tonic at measure 51. As is typical in fantasies, the performer is instructed to proceed directly to the second movement without pause.

The remaining two movements are more traditional in their structures. The second movement, in D-flat major (the enharmonic equivalent of C-sharp), follows the standard scherzo-trio-scherzo format, although the repeat of the first eight measures is written out and varied. A gentle mood is projected with subdued dynamics and minimal harmonic contrast: the scherzo lacks a strong move to the dominant, and the trio begins in the tonic. The most disruptive elements are the harmonic shifts during the second half of the trio and the syncopated accents on the third beats of measures throughout the movement.

The finale, in sonata form, provides a virtuosic conclusion. Marked *Presto agitato*, the movement establishes a restless quality with running sixteenth notes and rapid modulations. Following the dramatic opening, the exposition presents three contrasting thematic ideas (m. 20, m. 42, and m. 57) in the minor dominant (G-sharp). The last of these, the closing theme, shares characteristics with both of the preceding themes while subtly recalling the opening melody of the first movement. Fantasy qualities are also evident in the coda, with its sweeping arpeggiations, abrupt harmonic movement, and final evocation of the closing theme.

38

Wolfgang Amadeus Mozart

Requiem, *Dies irae, Tuba mirum,* and *Rex tremendae* (1791)

8CD: 4 / 52 – 59

3. Dies irae 52

4. Tuba mirum

5. Rex tremendae [59]

TEXT AND TRANSLATION

Verse

1. Dies irae, dies illa
Solvet saeclum in favilla,
Teste David cum Sibylla.

Day of anger, day of mourning
When to ashes all is burning
So spake David and the Sibyl.

2. Quantus tremor est futurus,
Quando judex est venturus,
Cuncta stricte discussurus!

Oh, what fear man's bosom rendeth.
When from Heaven the Judge descendeth.
On whose sentence all dependeth!

3. Tuba mirum spargens sonum
Per sepulchra regionum,
Coget omnes ante thronum.

Wondrous sound the trumpet flingeth,
Through earth's sepulchres it ringeth,
All before the throne it bringeth.

4. Mors stupebit et natura,
Cum resurget creatura,
Judicanti responsura.

Death with wonder is enchained,
When man from the dust regained,
Stands before the Judge arraigned.

5. Liber scriptus proferetur,
In quo totum continetur,
Unde mundus judicetur.

Now the record shall be cited,
Wherein all things stand indited,
Whence the world shall be requited.

6. Judex ergo cum sedebit,
Quidquid latet apparebit,
Nil inultum remanebit.

When to judgment all are bidden,
Nothing longer shall be hidden,
Not a trespass go unsmitten.

7. Quid sum miser tune dicturus?
Quem patronum rogatorus,
Cum vix justus sit securus?

What affliction mine exceeding?
Who shall stand forth for me pleading?
When the just man aid is needing?

8. Rex tremendae majestatis!
Qui salvandos salvas gratis!
Salve me, fons pietatis!

King of might and awe, defend met!
Freely Thy salvation send me!
Fount of mercy, save, befriend me!

Mozart began composing the Requiem Mass in 1791, but he was unable to complete the work prior to his untimely death. Franz Xavier Süssmayer, Mozart's composition student, finished the final movements on his teacher's behalf. In this setting of the traditional Latin text, Mozart incorporated numerous characteristics of traditional Baroque sacred music, including a monumental fugue. The resultant mixture of Baroque and Classical qualities is evident in the *Dies irae* movement.

The text of the *Dies irae* is a rhymed sequence by the thirteenth-century friar Thomas of Celano, an associate of Saint Francis of Assisi. It addresses with vivid imagery the day of reckoning. The mood of the text shifts from fear to wonderment and finally to a plea for salvation. This three-part division is maintained in Mozart's settings. The opening section, reflecting a Baroque influence, has no contrasting moods; the turbulence established in the opening measures is sustained until the final cadence. Fiery cascades of sixteenth notes, syncopated rhythms, homorhythmic vocal parts, the full sound of the orchestra, chromaticism, and harsh harmonies sustain the unrelenting energy and dark mood throughout. Also indicative of Baroque traditions is the word painting for "tremor," which is set with an undulating vocal line as if the singers were trembling.

The middle section, *Tuba mirum*, provides a strong contrast in musical forces and style. Employing only a quartet of solo singers, Mozart turns to an operatic sound with simple accompaniment patterns in the orchestra. The opening line ("the trumpet flingeth its wondrous sound") features a duet between a trombone and a bass singer. The tenor enters in a recitative style that reflects the text, "Mors stupebit et natura" ("Death and nature are stupefied"). The alto and soprano are given brief solos, and the four singers join for a closing quartet.

The final chorus, "Rex tremendae majestatis" ("King of tremendous majesty"), brings back the full choir and orchestra in a Grave tempo. The biting dotted rhythms recall the opening of a French overture, which has often been associated with kings. The chorus engages in four-part imitation over a dotted accompaniment, and the full sound of the choir and orchestra is maintained until the final quiet plea begins: "salva me!" ("save me!").

39

Franz Joseph Haydn

Die Schöpfung (*The Creation*), Part I, excerpts
(first performed 1799)

8CD: 3/ 58 – 60

58   **No. 12   Recitative (Uriel)**

Und Gott sprach: Es sei'n Lichter an der Feste des Himmels · *And God said: Let there be lights in the firmament of heaven*

Jah - re. Er mach - te die Ster - ne gleich - falls.

years. He made the stars al - so.

No. 13   Recitative (Uriel)

In vollem Glanze steiget jetzt die Sonne strahlend auf · *In splendour bright the sun is rising now*

In vol - lem Glan - ze stei - get jetzt die Son - ne strah - lend
In splen - dour bright is ri - sing now the sun and darts his

auf;   ein won - ne - vol - ler Bräu - ti - gam,
rays;   an am - 'rous, joy - ful, hap - py spouse,

Attacca

No. 14 Chorus and Trio

Die Himmel erzählen die Ehre Gottes · *The heavens are telling the glory of God*

Inspired by performances of Handel's oratorios in London, Haydn composed two oratorios late in his career. The first of these, *Die Schöpfung* (*The Creation*), draws its text from Genesis and Milton's *Paradise Lost*. Part I of the work deals with the first four days of Creation, concluding with two recitatives by Uriel (tenor soloist) and the chorus "Die Himmel erzählen" ("The Heavens are telling"). The first recitative is accompanied by the basso continuo (*secco*) and is characterized by a limited range, repeated notes, and a sparse accompaniment. The second recitative, which opens with a stunning orchestral crescendo depicting the rising sun, is accompanied by the orchestra (*accompagnato*), treats the melodic line more freely, and contains several notable examples of word painting.

"Die Himmel erzählen" alternates three sections for chorus with two passages sung by the trio of angels. The first choral section presents three four-measure phrases **(A-B-B)**, which serve as material for the other choral and solo sections. The energy of the movement, which builds from the simple beginning through more complicated textures, climaxes with a fugal passage and a final choral statement accompanied by brass and timpani.

40

Wolfgang Amadeus Mozart

Le nozze di Figaro (*The Marriage of Figaro*),
Overture and Act I, Scenes 6 and 7 (1786)

8CD: 4/ 60 – 72
4CD: 2/ 49 – 56

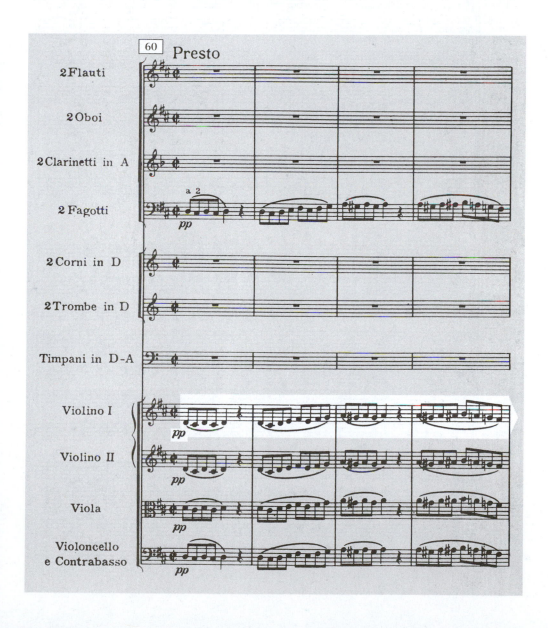

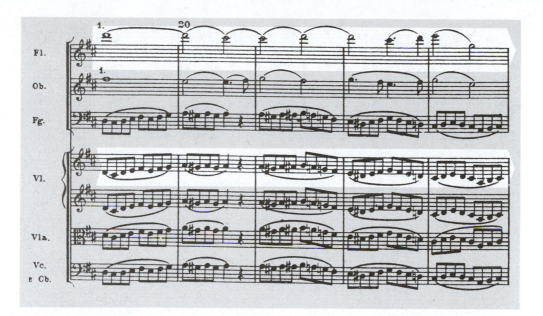

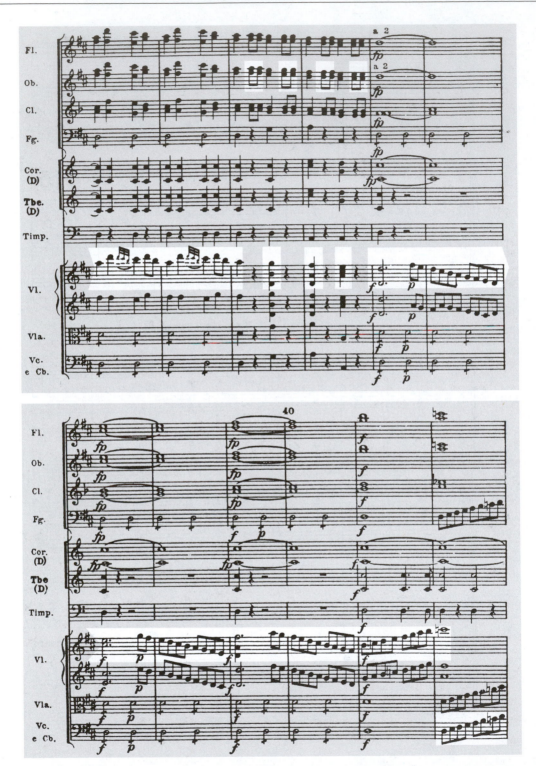

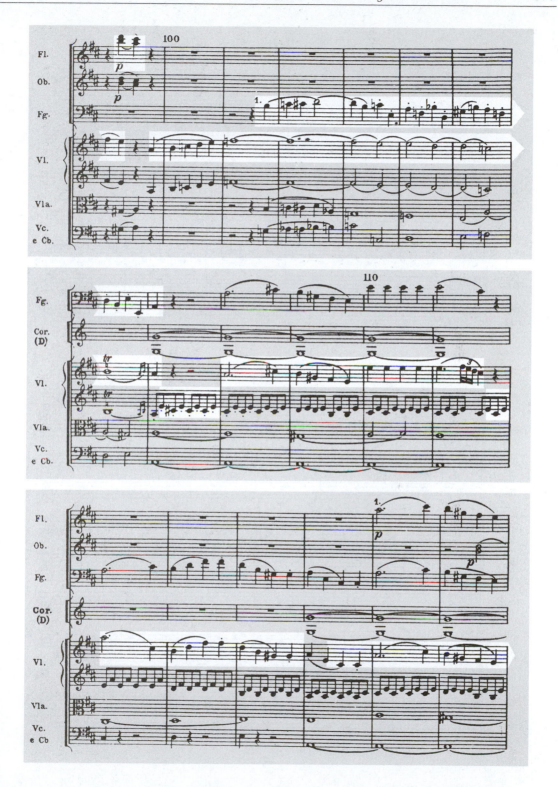

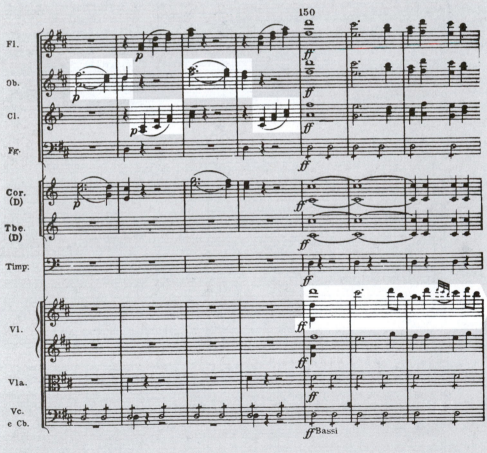

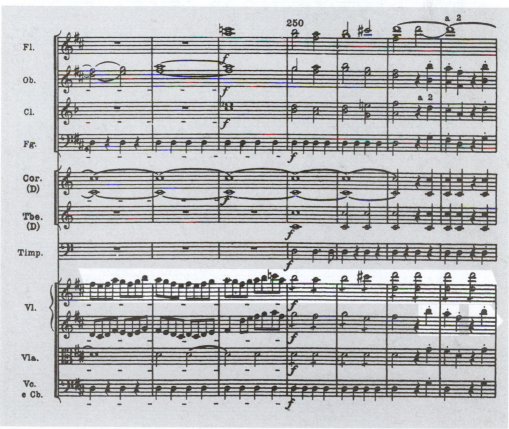

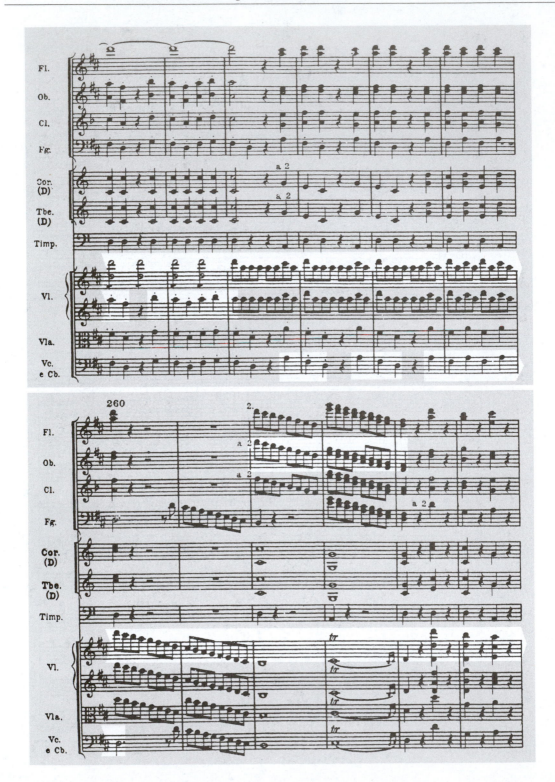

No. 6. "Non so più cosa son, cosa faccio"

Recitative

Susanna (*timidly*)

rò; di con-dur me-co Fi-ga-ro de-sti-na-i. Si-gnor, se o-
Lon-don, and I ar-ranged for Fi-ga-ro to go with me. If I dared

Count (*rising*)

sas-si— Par-la, par-la, mia ca-ra, e con quel drit-to ch'og-gi pren-di su
ask you— Ask me, ask me, my dar-ling, and with that right you ex-ert o-ver

(*tenderly, and trying to take her hand again*)   **Susanna**

me, fin-chè tu vi-vi chie-di, im-po-ni, pre-scri-vi. La-scia-te-mi, si-
me, now and al-ways, ask me, com-pel me, com-mand me! I do not wish that

(*angrily*)

gnor, drit-ti non pren-do, non ne vò, non ne in-ten-do.
right, I ask no priv-i-lege, I don't want to ex-ert it;

Count

Oh, me in-fe-li-ce! Ah no, Su-san-na, io ti vò far fe-
I'm so un-hap-py! No, no, Su-san-na, I want you to be

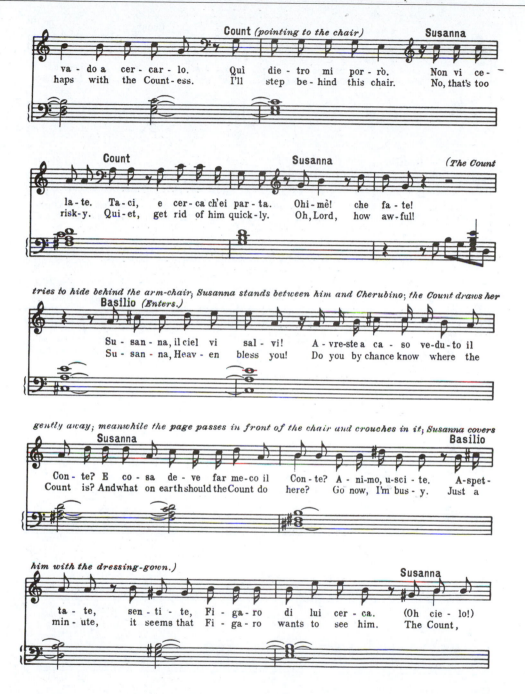

Count *(pointing to the chair)*

Susanna

va - do a cer - car - lo. Quì die - tro mi por - rò. Non vi ce -
haps with the Count - ess. I'll step be - hind this chair. No, that's too

Count

Susanna

(The Count

la - te. Ta - ci, e cer - ca ch'ei par - ta. Ohi - mè! che fa - te!
risk - y. Qui - et, get rid of him quick - ly. Oh, Lord, how aw - ful!

tries to hide behind the arm-chair; Susanna stands between him and Cherubino; the Count draws her

Basilio *(Enters.)*

Su - san - na, il ciel vi sal - vi! A - vre - ste a ca - so ve - du - to il
Su - san - na, Heav - en bless you! Do you by chance know where the

gently away; meanwhile the page passes in front of the chair and crouches in it; Susanna covers

Susanna

Basilio

Con - te? E co - sa de - ve far me - co il Con - te? A - ni - mo, u - sci - te. A - spet -
Count is? And what on earth should the Count do here? Go now, I'm bus - y. Just a

him with the dressing-gown.)

Susanna

ta - te, sen - ti - te, Fi - ga - ro di lui cer - ca. (Oh cie - lo!)
min - ute, it seems that Fi - ga - ro wants to see him. The Count,

che s'il Con - te s'ac-cor - ge, e sul tal pun - to, sa - pe - te, e-gli è u - na
that if the Count should take no-tice you can im - ag - ine, in that case, what's bound to

Susanna

be - stia. Scel-le - ra - to! e per-chè an - da - te voi tai men-zo - gne spar-
hap - pen. Oh, you li - ar! Have you noth - ing more to do than to spread vi-cious

Basilio

gen - do? Io! che in-giu-sti - zia! Quel che com-pro io ven - do, a
gos - sip? I! You're mis-tak - en, I just sell what I pur - chase, I

quel che tut - ti di - co - no, io non ci ag - giun-go un pe - lo.
ech - o what they all say, not add - ing in the slight-est.

Count (*Steps forward.*) **Basilio** **Susanna**

Co - me! che di-con tut - ti? Oh bel - la! Oh cie - lo!
Real - ly! What are they say - ing? (De - light - ful!) Ah, Heav - ens!

No. 7. "Cosa sento! Tosto andate"

Count *(to Basilio)*

Co - sa sen - to! To - sto an - da - te,
That's the lim - it! Go this min - ute,

e scac-cia - te il se - dut - tor, to - sto an -
find the cul-prit and throw him out, go and

da - te, e scac-cia - te il se - dut - tor. In mal pun - to
find him, and throw the cul - prit out. How ill - cho - sen

Basilio

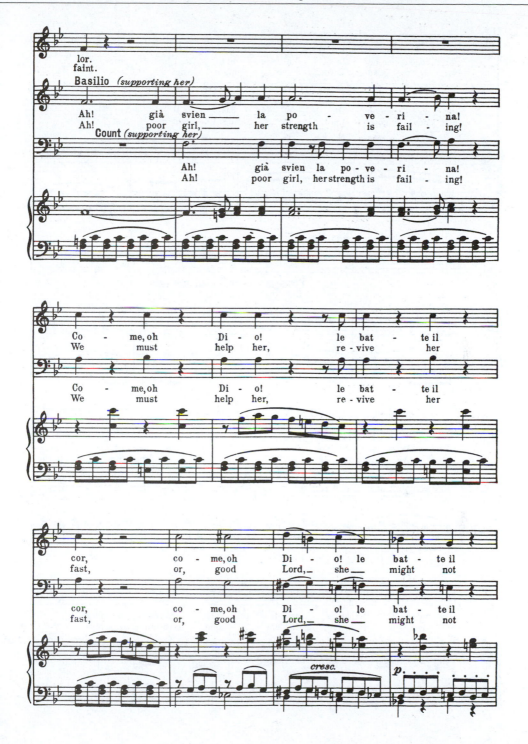

a tempo

Ed al - zan - do, pian, pia - ni - no, il tap - pe - to al
When I gent - ly drew the cov - er from the ta - ble I

(Showing how he found the page, he lifts the dressing-

ta - vo - li - no, ve - do il pag - gio.
found be - neath it Che - ru - bi - no!

Susanna *(agitated)*

Ah! cru - de stel - le!
Ah, this is aw - ful!

gown from the chair and discovers Cherubino.)
(astonished)

Ah! co - sa veg - gio!
Ha! What does this mean?

72 56

Susanna

Ac - ca -
Noth - ing

Basilio *(laughing sardonically)*

Ah! me - glio an - co - ra!
Ah, this is price - less!

Count

O - ne - stis - si - ma si - gno - ra!
Now at last my eyes are o - pen!

no! ah, no! giu-sti Dei, che mai sa-rà, che mai sa-
no! ah, no! This af-fair is out of hand; how will this

fan tut-te_ le_ bel-le, non c'è al-cu-na_ no-vi-
way all wo-men do it, they will nev-er_ show their

ma _ si-gno-ra! or ca-pi-sco co-me
eyes_ are o-pen, now I see_ how mat-ters

rà! ac - ca - der non può di peg-gio,
end? Noth - ing worse than this could hap-pen,

tà, co - sì fan tut - te le bel - le,
hand. That's the way all wo - men do it,

va, o - ne - stis - si - ma si - gno-ra,
stand. Now at last _ my eyes are o - pen,

giu - sti   Dei,__ che__ mai   sa - rà!
no   one   knows how__ this will   end.

(to the Count, with malice)

non c'è al - cu - na__ ño - vi - tà. Ah, del pag - gio
they will   nev - er__ show their hand. What I told you

or   ca - pi - sco   co - me   va!
now   I   see __ how__ mat - ters   stand.

cresc.   *p*

quel che ho det - to,   e - ra   so - lo   un mio so -
was   a   ru - mor,   mere sus - pi - cion with no foun -

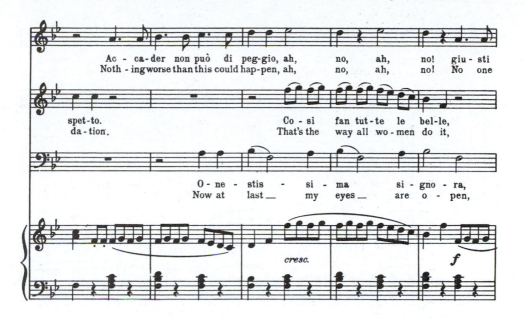

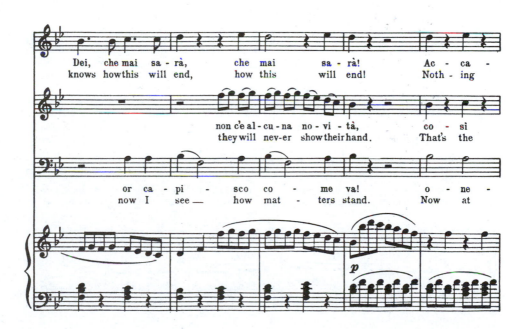

der   non può di peg-gio,   giu - sti Dei,— che—
worse   than this could hap-pen, no   one knows how—

fan   tut - te le bel - le,   non c'è al - cu - na—
way   all wo - men do it,   they will   nev - er—

stis - si - ma si - gno-ra,   or ca - pi - sco—
last—   my eyes are o - pen, now I   see— how—

cresc.

mai sa - rà, giu - sti Dei,— che— mai sa - rà, giu - sti
this will end, no   one knows how— this will end, this af -

no - vi - tà, non c'è al - cu - na— no - vi - tà, non c'è al -
show their hand, they will nev - er— show their hand, they will

co - me va, or ca - pi - sco— co - me va, or ca -
mat - ters stand, now I see— how— mat - ters stand, now I

p   *sfp*   *cresc.*   *p*

Le nozze di Figaro (The Marriage of Figaro) (1786) is a brilliant comic opera (*opera buffa*) based on a libretto by Lorenzo da Ponte. Adapted from a controversial Beaumarchais play, the opera sparkles with wit and satire. While the story is basically a bedroom farce, Mozart creates a theatrical masterpiece with his depth of characterization, sublime music, and innovative ensemble treatment.

The overture, which establishes the quick pace and jovial mood of the opera, is set in a modified sonata-allegro form. The exposition and recapitulation are tuneful and clearly delineated, but the development section is omitted. Additional modifications can be seen in the absence of repeats in the exposition and the lack of closure at the end, when the overture segues into the first scene.

The music for Act I, Scene 6, begins with Cherubino's ardent aria "Non so più." Cherubino is a young boy who has discovered women. In love with the Countess, he sings a song about love to her servant Susanna. In keeping with his youthful character, the song maintains simplicity of form **(A-B-A-C)** and texture. The pulsating string accompaniment suggests the excited, breathless state of Cherubino. Some of the humor in this scene stems from Mozart's assignment of a mezzo-soprano to the character of Cherubino, one of the most amusing and enjoyable examples of a "trouser role" in all of opera.

In the delightful *secco* recitative that follows, the Count comes to woo Susanna. Cherubino, not wanting to be seen, takes refuge behind a large chair. The entrance of Basilio, the voice teacher, prompts the Count to hide behind the same chair, while Cherubino stealthily climbs into the chair under a dress. Basilio's idle chatter eventually angers the Count, and he comes out of hiding—to the delight of the music master.

Act I, Scene 7, is a trio, one of several celebrated ensembles in the opera. In these musical numbers, Mozart is able to create operatic scenes in which the drama is advanced without sacrificing the music. The trio for Susanna, the Count, and Basilio can be seen as an extended sonata-allegro form. After the initial statements in B-flat major, Susanna attempts to distract the men from Cherubino's presence by pretending to faint. Mozart supports her diversion with a modulation to the dominant as the men admire her figure. But Susanna's efforts are in vain, and the Count uncovers Cherubino while relating an earlier episode about the young man. The opening material returns, and now Susanna is unable to detour the Count and Basilio from the tonic key.

Appendix A

Reading a Musical Score

Clefs

The music for some instruments is written in clefs other than the familiar treble and bass. In the following example, middle C is shown in the four clefs used in orchestral scores:

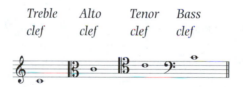

The *alto clef* is primarily used in viola parts. The *tenor clef* is employed for cello, bassoon, and trombone parts when these instruments play in a high register.

Transposing Instruments

The music for some instruments is customarily written at a pitch different from its actual sound. The following list, with examples, shows the main transposing instruments and the degree of transposition. (In some modern works—such as the Stravinsky example included in volume two of this anthology—all instruments are written at their sounding pitch.)

Instrument	Transposition	Written note	Actual sound
Piccolo Celesta	sounds an octave higher than written		
Trumpet in F	sounds a fourth higher than written		
Trumpet in E	sounds a major third higher than written		
Clarinet in E♭ Trumpet in E♭	sounds a minor third higher than written		
Trumpet in D Clarinet in D	sounds a major second higher than written		
Clarinet in B♭ Trumpet in B♭ Cornet in B♭ French horn in B♭, alto	sounds a major second lower than written		
Clarinet in A Trumpet in A Cornet in A	sounds a minor third lower than written		
French horn in G Alto flute	sounds a fourth lower than written		
English horn French horn in F	sounds a fifth lower than written		
French horn in E	sounds a minor sixth lower than written		
French horn in E♭ Alto saxophone	sounds a major sixth lower than written		
French horn in D	sounds a minor seventh lower than written		
Contrabassoon French horn in C Double bass	sounds an octave lower than written		
Bass clarinet in B♭ Tenor saxophone (written in treble clef)	sounds a major ninth lower than written		
Tenor saxophone (written in bass clef)	sounds a major second lower than written		
Bass clarinet in A (written in treble clef)	sounds a minor tenth lower than written		
Bass clarinet in A (written in bass clef)	sounds a minor third lower than written		
Baritone saxophone in B♭ (written in treble clef)	sounds an octave and a major sixth lower than written		

Appendix B

Instrument Names and Abbreviations

The following tables set forth the English, Italian, German, and French names used for the various musical instruments in these scores, and their respective abbreviations (when used). Latin voice designations and a table of the foreign-language names for scale degrees and modes are also provided.

Woodwinds

English	Italian	German	French
Piccolo (Picc.)	Flauto piccolo (Fl. Picc.)	Kleine Flöte (Kl. Fl.)	Petitie flûte
Flute (Fl.)	Flauto (Fl.); Flauto grande (Fl. gr.)	Grosse Flöte (Gr. Fl.)	Flûte (Fl.)
Alto flute	Flauto contralto (fl. c-alto)	Altflöte	Flûte en sol
Oboe (Ob.)	Oboe (Ob.)	Hoboe (Hb.); Oboe (Ob.)	Hautbois (Hb.)
English horn (E. H.)	Corno inglese (C. or Cor. ingl., C.i.)	Englisches Horn (E. H.)	Cor anglais (C. A.)
E♭ clarinet	Clarinetto piccolo (clar. picc.)		
Clarinet (C., Cl., Clt., Clar.)	Clarinetto (Cl., Clar.)	Klarinette (Kl.)	Clarinette (Cl.)
Bass clarinet (B. Cl.)	Clarinetto basso (Cl. b., Cl. basso, Clar. basso)	Bass Klarinette (Bkl.)	Clarinette basse (Cl. bs.)
Bassoon (Bsn., Bssn.)	Fagotto (Fag., Fg.)	Fagott (Fag., Fg.)	Basson (Bssn.)

English	Italian	German	French
Contrabassoon (C. Bsn.)	Contrafagotto (Cfg., C. Fag., Cont. F.)	Kontrafagott (Kfg.)	Contrebasson (C. bssn.)
Alto saxophone Tenor saxophone Baritone saxophone	Sassofone	Saxophon	Saxophone

Brass

English	Italian	German	French
French horn (Hr., Hn.)	Corno (Cor., C.)	Horn (Hr.) [*pl.* Hörner (Hrn.)]	Cor; Cor à pistons
Trumpet (Tpt., Trpt., Trp., Tr.)	Tromba (Tr.) [*pl.* Tbe.]	Trompete (Tr., Trp.)	Trompette (Tr.)
Trumpet in D	Tromba piccola (Tr. picc.)		
Cornet	Cornetta	Kornett	Cornet à pistons (C. à p., Pist.)
Trombone (Tr., Tbe., Trb., Trm., Trbe.)	Trombone [pl. Tromboni (Tbni., Trni.)]	Posaune (Ps., Pos.)	Trombone (Tr.)
Bass trombone Tuba (Tb.)	Tuba (Tb., Tba.)	Tuba (Tb.) [*also* Basstuba (Btb.)]	Tuba (Tb.)
Ophicleide	Oficleide	Ophikleide	Ophicléide

Percussion

English	Italian	German	French
Percussion (Perc.)	Percussione	Schlagzeug (Schlag.)	Batterie (Batt.)
Kettledrums (K. D.)	Timpani (Timp., Tp.)	Pauken (Pk.)	Timbales (Timb.)
Snare drum (S. D.)	Tamburo piccolo (Tamb. picc.) Tamburo militare (Tamb. milit.)	Kleine Trommel (Kl. Tr.)	Caisse claire (C. cl.); Caisse roulante Tambour militaire (Tamb. milit.)
Bass drum (B. drum)	Gran cassa (Gr. Cassa, Gr. C., G. C.); Tamburo grande (T. gr.)	Grosse Trommel (Gr. Tr.)	Grosse caisse (Gr. c.)
Cymbals (Cym., Cymb.)	Piatti (P., Ptti., Piat.)	Becken (Beck.)	Cymbales (Cym.)
Tam-Tam (Tam.-T.)			
Tambourine (Tamb.)	Tamburino (Tamb.)	Schellentrommel; Tamburin	Tambour de Basque. (T. de B., Tamb. de Basque)

English	Italian	German	French
Triangle (Trgl., Tri.)	Triangolo (Trgl.)	Triangel	Triangle (Triang.)
Glockenspiel (Glocken.)	Campanelli (Cmp.)	Glockenspiel	Carillon
Bells; Chimes	Campane (Cmp.)	Glocken	Cloches
Antique cymbals	Crotali; Piatti antichi	Antike Zimbeln	Crotales; Cymbales antiques
Sleigh bells	Sonagli (Son.)	Schellen	Grelots
Xylophone (Xyl.)	Xilofono	Xylophon	Xylophone
Cowbells		Herdenglocken	
Crash cymbal			Grande cymbale chinoise
Siren			Sirène
Lion's roar			Tambour à corde
Slapstick			Fouet
Wood blocks			Blocs chinois

Strings

English	Italian	German	French
Violin (V., Vl., Vln., Vi., Vn.)	Violino (V., Vl., Vln.)	Violine (V., Vl., Vln.); Geige (Gg.)	Violon (V., Vl., Vln.)
Viola (Va., Vl.) [*pl.* Vas.]	Viola (Va., Vla.) [*pl.* Viole (Vle.)]	Bratsche (Br.)	Alto (A.)
Violoncello; Cello (Vcl., Vc.)	Violoncello (Vc., Vlc., Vcllo.)	Violoncell (Vc., Vlc.)	Violoncelle (Vc.)
Double bass (D. Bs.)	Contrabasso (Cb., C. B.) [*pl.* Contrabassi or Bassi (C. Bassi, Bi.)]	Kontrabass (Kb.)	Contrebasse (C. B.)

Other Instruments

English	Italian	German	French
Harp (Hp., Hrp.)	Arpa (A., Arp.)	Harfe (Hrf.)	Harpe (Hp.)
Piano	Pianoforte (P.-f., Pft.)	Klavier	Piano
Celesta (Cel.)			
Harpsichord	Cembalo	Cembalo	Clavecin
Fortepiano (Fp.)	Fortepiano		
Harmonium (Harmon.)			
Organ (Org.)	Organo	Orgel	Orgue
Guitar	Chitarra	Gitarre (Git.)	Guitare
Mandoline (Mand.)			
Continuous bass, thorough bass (cont.)	Basso continuo (B.C.)	Generalbass	Basse continue

Voice Designations

English	Latin	Italian
Soprano (S.), Treble	Cantus (C.), Superius	Canto
Alto (A.)	Altus, Contratenor	Alto, Contratenore
Tenor (T.)	Tenor	Tenore
Bass (B.)	Bassus, Contratenor Bassus	Basso
Fifth voice	Quintus (V, 5)	Quinto
Sixth voice	Sextus (VI, 6)	Sexto

Tenor: lowest voice in medieval polyphony
Triplum: third voice above Tenor in medieval polyphony
Duplum: second voice above Tenor in medieval polyphony

Name of Scale Degrees

English	Italian	German	French
C	do	C	ut
C-sharp	do diesis	Cis	ut dièse
D-flat	re bemolle	Des	ré bémol
D	re	D	ré
D-sharp	re diesis	Dis	ré dièse
E-flat	mi bemolle	Es	mi bémol
E	mi	E	mi
E-sharp	mi diesis	Eis	mi dièse
F-flat	fa bemolle	Fes	fa bémol
F	fa	F	fa
F-sharp	fa diesis	Fis	fa dièse
G-flat	sol bemolle	Ges	sol bémol
G	sol	G	sol
G-sharp	sol diesis	Gis	sol dièse
A-flat	la bemolle	As	la bémol
A	la	A	la
A-sharp	la diesis	Ais	la dièse
B-flat	si bemolle	B	si bémol
B	si	H	si
B-sharp	si diesis	His	si dièse
C-flat	do bemolle	Ces	ut bémol

Modes

English	Italian	German	French
major	maggiore	dur	majeur
minor	minore	moll	mineur

Medieval and Renaissance Instruments Heard in Norton Recordings

Strings, bowed

rebec
vielle (fiddle)
viola da gamba

Strings, plucked

harp
lute
psaltery

Strings, struck

dulcimer

Winds

cornetto
3-hole pipe
recorder
sackbut
shawm

Percussion

tabor

Keyboard

harpsichord
organ

A Note on Baroque Instruments

In the Baroque era, certain instruments that are not used in today's modern orchestra were required by the composers; the following list defines these terms.

Clarino (*clarini*): A Baroque or Classical-era trumpet; also the upper range of a Baroque trumpet, or a style of trumpet-playing on a natural trumpet.

Continuo (*Cont.* or *B.C.*): A method of indicating an accompanying part by the bass notes only, together with figures (numbers) designating the chords to be played above them (figured bass). In general practice, the chords are played on a harpsichord or organ, while a viola da gamba or cello doubles the bass notes.

Oboe d'amore: In Bach's Cantata No. 80, this term indicates an alto oboe.

Ripieno (*Rip.*): Tutti, the full ensemble that alternates with the solo instrument or solo group (*Concertino*).

Taille (*Tail.*): In Bach's Cantata No. 80, this term indicates a tenor oboe or English horn.

Violino piccolo: A small violin, tuned a fourth higher than the standard violin.

Violone (*V.*): A string instrument intermediate in size between the cello and the double bass. (In modern performances, the double bass is commonly substituted.)

Appendix C
Glossary of Musical Terms Used in the Scores

The following glossary is not intended to be a complete dictionary of musical terms, nor is knowledge of all these terms necessary to follow the scores in this book. However, as listeners gain experience in following scores, they will find it useful and interesting to understand the composer's directions with regard to tempo, dynamics, and methods of performance.

In most cases, compound terms have been broken down and defined separately, as they often recur in varying combinations. A few common foreign-language words are included in addition to the musical terms. Note that names and abbreviations for instruments and for scale degrees will be found in Appendix B.

a The phrases *a 2*, *a 3* (etc.) indicate the number of parts to be played by 2, 3 (etc.) players; when a simple number (1, 2, etc.) is placed over a part, it indicates that only the first (second, etc.) player in that group should play.

aber But.

a cappella In the manner of the chapel, as in unaccompanied choral singing.

accelerando (*accel.*) Growing faster.

accordato, accordez Tune the instrument as specified.

adagio Slow, leisurely.

affettuoso With emotion.

affrettare (*affrett.*) Hastening a little.

agitando, agitato Agitated, excited.

air The English or French equivalent of the Italian aria.

al fine "The end"; an indication to return to the start of a piece and to repeat it only to the point marked "fine."

alla breve Indicates two beats to a measure, at a rather quick tempo.

allargando (*allarg.*) Growing broader.

alla turca In the Turkish style.

alle, alles All, every, each.

allegretto A moderately fast tempo (between *allegro* and *andante*).

allegro A rapid tempo (between *allegretto* and *presto*).

allein Alone, solo.

Alleluia A movement from the Proper of the Mass sung just before the reading of the Gospel, with a long melisma on the last syllable of the word "Alleluia."

allmählich Gradually (*allmählich wieder gleichmässig fliessend werden*, gradually becoming even-flowing again).

alta, alto, altus (*A*). The deeper of the two main divisions of women's (or boys') voices.

am Steg On the bridge (of a string instrument).

ancora Again.

andante A moderately slow tempo (between *adagio* and *allegretto*).

andantino A moderately slow tempo.

Anfang Beginning, initial.

anima Spirit, animation.

animando With increasing animation.

animant, animato, animé, animez Animated.

aperto Indicates open notes on the horn, open strings, and undampened piano notes.

a piacere The execution of the passage is left to the performer's discretion.

appassionato Impassioned.

appena Scarcely, hardly.

apprensivo Apprehensive.

archet Bow.

archi Bowed string instruments.

arco Played with the bow.

arditamente Boldly.

aria Lyric song for solo voice with orchestral accompaniment, generally expressing intense emotion; found in operas, cantatas, and oratorios.

arpeggiando, arpeggiato (*arpegg.*) Played in harp style; i.e., the notes of the chord played in quick succession rather than simultaneously.

assai Very.

assez Fairly, rather.

attacca Begin what follows without pausing.

a tempo At the original tempo.

auf dem On the (as in *auf dem* G, on the G string).

Ausdruck Expression.

ausdrucksvoll With expression.

äusserst Extreme, utmost.

avec With.

bachetta, bachetti Drumsticks (*bachetti di spugna*, sponge-headed drumsticks).

baguettes Drumsticks (*baguettes de bois*, wooden drumsticks; *baguettes d'éponge*, sponge-headed drumsticks).

ballad opera English comic opera, usually featuring spoken dialogue alternating with songs set to popular tunes.

bass, bassi, basso, bassus (*B.*) The lowest male voice.

basso ostinato Repeated bass; also *ground bass*.

basso seguente The bottom voice of a Renaissance or early Baroque work, played by an organ or harpsichord in the manner of a basso continuo.

battere, battuta, battuto (*batt.*) To beat.

Becken Cymbals.

bedeutend bewegter With significantly more movement.

beider Hände With both hands.

ben Very.

bewegt Agitated.

bewegter More agitated.

binary form Two part (**A-B**) form, normally with each section repeated.

bisbigliando, bispiglando (*bis.*) Whispering.

bis zum schluss dieser Szene To the end of this scene.

blasen Blow.

Blech Brass instruments.

Bogen (*bog.*) Played with the bow.

bois Woodwind.

bouché Muted.

breit Broadly.

breiter More broadly.

brio Spirit, vivacity.

Brustpositiv A division of an organ normally based on 2' or 4' pitch.

cadenza (*cad., cadenz.*) An extended passage for solo instrument in free, improvisatory style, performed at the end of an aria or concerto movement.

calando (*cal.*) Diminishing in volume and speed.

calma, calmo Calm, calmly.

cantabile (cant.) In a singing style.

cantando In a singing manner.

cantata Vocal genre for solo singers, chorus, and instruments based on a lyric or dramatic poetic narrative;

generally consists of several movements including recitatives, arias, and ensemble numbers.

canto Voice (as in *col canto*, a direction for the accompaniment to follow the solo part in tempo and expression).

cantus An older designation for the highest part in a vocal work.

cantus firmus Fixed song; a preexistent melody used as the structural basis of a polyphonic composition.

capriccio Capriciously, whimsically.

chaconne A kind of ground bass form with repeated harmonic progression.

changez Change (usually an instruction to retune a string or an instrument).

chanson French polyphonic song, especially from the Middle Ages or Renaissance, set to courtly or popular poetry.

chiuso See *gestopft*.

chorale A congregational hymn in the German Lutheran Church; sometimes used as the basis for large-scale compositions.

chromatisch Chromatic.

circa (*c.*) About, approximately.

closed The second of two endings in a secular medieval work, usually cadencing on the final.

coda A concluding section extraneous to the form; a formal closing gesture.

col, colla, coll' With the.

colore Colored.

come prima, come sopra As at first, as previously.

commodo Comfortable, easy.

con With.

concertino The solo group in a Baroque concerto grosso.

concerto Instrumental genre in several movements for solo instrument (or instrumental group) and orchestra.

corda String; for example, *seconda* (*2a*) *corda* is the second string (the A string on the violin).

corto Short, brief.

crescendo (*cresc.*) An increase in volume.

cuivré Played with a harsh, blaring tone.

da capo (*D.C.*) Repeat from the beginning.

da capo aria Lyric song in ternary (**A-B-A**) form, commonly found in operas, cantatas, and oratorios.

dal segno (*D.S.*) Repeat from the sign.

Dämpfer (*Dpf.*) Mutes.

dazu In addition to that, for that purpose.

de, des, die Of, from.

début Beginning

deciso Determined, resolute.

decrescendo (*decresc., decr.*) A decreasing of volume.

dehors Outside.

delicatamente Delicately.

delicatissimamente Very delicately.

dem To the.

détaché With a broad, vigorous bow stroke, each note bowed singly.

deutlich Distinctly.

d'exécution Performance.

diminuendo, diminuer (*dim., dimin.*) A decreasing of volume.

distinto Distinct, clear.

divisés, divisi (*div.*) Divided; indicates that the instrumental group should be divided into two parts to play the passage in question.

dolce Sweetly and softly.

dolcemente Sweetly.

dolcissimo (*dolciss.*) Very sweetly.

Doppelgriff Double stop.

double exposition In the concerto, twofold statement of the themes, once by the orchestra and once by the soloist.

doux Sweetly.

drängend Pressing on.

dreifach Triple.

dreitaktig Three beats to a measure.

dur Major, as in *G dur* (G major).

durée Duration.

e, et And.

eilen To hurry.

ein One, a.

elegante Elegant, graceful.

energico Energetically.

espansione Expansion, broadening.

espressione With expression.

espressivo (*espr., espress.*) Expressively.

estampie Dance form popular in France and Italy in the thirteenth and fourteenth centuries.

etwas Somewhat, rather.

expressif Expressively.

facile Simple.

fagotto Bassoon; an organ reed stop.

fiati Wind instruments.

fin, fine End, close.

finale Final movement or section of a work.

finalis Pitch on which a melody ends in a church mode; the final pitch.

Flatterzunge, flutter tongue A special tonguing technique for wind instruments, producing a rapid, trill-like sound.

flebile Feeble, plaintive, mournful.

fliessend Flowing.

forte (f) Loud.

fortepiano (fp) Loud followed immediately by soft.

fortissimo (ff) Very loud (*fff* indicates a still louder dynamic).

forza Force.

forzando (f_z) Forced, strongly accented.

fou Frantic.

frappez To strike.

frei Freely.

freihäng., freihängendes Hanging freely. An indication to the percussionist to let the cymbals vibrate freely.

frisch Fresh, lively.

fugue Polyphonic form popular in the Baroque era in which one or more themes are developed by imitative counterpoint.

furioso Furiously.

ganz Entirely, altogether.

Ganzton Whole tone.

gedämpft (ged.) Muted.

geheimnisvoll Mysteriously.

geschlagen Pulsating.

gestopft (gest.) Stopping the notes of a horn; that is, the hand is placed in the bell of the horn to produce a muffled sound. Also *chiuso*.

geteilt (get.) Divided; indicates that the instrumental group should be divided into two parts to play the passage in question.

getragen Sustained.

gewöhnlich As usual.

gigue English Baroque dance in compound meter; a standard movement of the Baroque suite.

giocoso Humorous.

giusto Moderately.

glissando (gliss.) Rapid scales produced by sliding the fingers over all the strings.

Gloria The second musical movement of the Mass Ordinary.

gradamente Gradually.

grande Large, great.

grandioso Grandiose.

grave Slow, solemn; deep, low.

grazioso Gracefully.

Gregorian chant Monophonic melody with free-flowing, unmeasured line; liturgical chant of the Roman Catholic Church. Also *plainchant*.

grosser Auftakt Big upbeat.

ground bass A repeating melody, usually in the bass, throughout a vocal or instrumental composition.

gut Good, well.

Hälfte Half.

Hauptzeitmass Original tempo.

hervortreten Prominent.

hoch High, nobly.

Holz Woodwinds.

Holzschlägel Wooden drumstick.

hornpipe Country dance of the British Isles, often in lively triple meter; an optional dance in the Baroque suite.

im gleichen Rhythmus In the same rhythm.

immer Always.

in Oktaven In octaves.

insensibilmente Slightly, imperceptibly.

intensa Intensely.

istesso tempo Duration of beat remains unaltered despite meter change.

jeu Playful.

jubilus The extended melisma sung to the final syllable of the word

"Alleluia," in the Alleluia of the Proper of the Mass.

jusqu'à Until.

kadenzieren To cadence.

klagend Lamenting.

kleine Little.

klingen To sound.

komisch bedeutsam Very humorously.

kurz Short.

Kyrie The first movement of the Mass Ordinary; text is Greek in origin.

langsam Slow.

langsamer Slower.

languendo, langueur Languor.

l'archet See archet.

largamente Broadly.

larghetto Slightly faster than *largo*.

largo A very slow tempo.

lasci, lassen To abandon.

lebhaft Lively.

lebhafter Livelier.

legatissimo A more forceful indication of *legato*.

legato Performed without any perceptible interruption between notes.

légèrement, leggieramente Lightly.

leggiero (*legg.*) Light and graceful.

legno The wood of the bow (*col legno gestrich*, played with the wood).

lent Slow.

lentamente Slowly.

lento A slow tempo (between *andante* and *largo*).

l.h. Abbreviation for "left hand."

ligature A notational device that combines two or more notes in a single symbol.

liricamente Lyrically.

loco Indicates a return to the written pitch, following a passage played an octave higher or lower than written.

lontano Distant.

Luftpause Pause for breath.

lunga Long, sustained.

lusingando Caressing.

ma, mais But.

madrigal Renaissance polyphonic secular work for voices set to a short, lyric love poem originating in Italy but also popular in England.

maestoso Majestic.

maggiore Major mode.

marcatissimo (*marcatiss.*) With very marked emphasis.

marcato (*marc.*) Marked, with emphasis.

marschmässig, nicht eilen Moderate-paced march, not rushed.

marziale Military, martial, march-like.

mässig Moderately.

mässiger More moderately.

même Same.

meno Less.

mezza voce Restrained, with half voice.

mezzo forte (*mf*) Moderately loud.

mezzo piano (*mp*) Moderately soft.

mindestens At least.

minore Minor mode.

minuet and trio **A-B-A** form (**A** = minuet; **B** = trio) in moderate triple meter; often the third movement of the Classical multimovement cycle.

misterioso Mysterious.

misura Measured.

mit With.

moderatissimo A more forceful indication of *moderato*.

moderato, modéré At a moderate tempo.

moins Less.

molto Very, much.

mordenti Biting, pungent.

morendo Dying away.

mormorato Murmured.

mosso Rapid.

motet Polyphonic vocal genre, secular in the Middle Ages but sacred or devotional thereafter.

moto Motion.

mouvement (*mouv., mouvt.*) Tempo.

muta, mutano Change the tuning of the instrument as specified.

nach After.

naturalezza A natural, unaffected manner.

neuen New.

neume A notational sign used in chant to designate pitch.

nicht Not.

niente Nothing.

nimmt To take; to seize.

noch Still.

non Not.

nuovo New.

obere, oberer (*ob.*) Upper, leading.

Oberwerk Secondary division of the organ, with pipes behind the player.

oder langsamer Or slower.

offen Open.

ohne Without.

ondeggiante Undulating movement of the bow, which produces a tremolo effect.

open The first ending in a secular medieval piece, usually cadencing on a pitch other than the final.

oratorio Large-scale dramatic genre originating in the Baroque, based on a text of religious or serious character and performed by solo voices, chorus, and orchestra; similar to opera but without scenery, costumes, or action.

ordinario (*ord.*, *ordin.*) In the usual way (generally canceling an instruction to play using some special technique).

organum Earliest kind of polyphonic music, which developed from the custom of adding voices above a plainchant.

ossia An alternative (usually easier) version of a passage.

ostinato A short melodic, rhythmic, or harmonic pattern repeated throughout a work or a section of one.

ôtez vite les sourdines Remove the mutes quickly.

ottoni Brass.

ouvert Open.

overture An introductory movement, as in an opera or oratorio, often presenting melodies from arias to come.

parte Part (colla parte, the accompaniment is to follow the soloist in tempo).

passionato Passionately.

pastourelle A genre of troubadour or trouvère song built on a debate between a shepherdess and a knight.

Paukenschlägel Timpani stick.

pavillons en l'air An indication to the player of a wind instrument to raise the bell of the instrument upward.

pedal, pedale (*ped.*, *P.*) (1) In piano music, indicates that the damper pedal should be depressed; an asterisk indicates the point of release (brackets below the music are also used to indicate pedaling). (2) On an organ, the pedals are a keyboard played with the feet.

per During.

perdendosi Gradually dying away.

pesante Heavily.

peu Little, a little.

piacevole Agreeable, pleasant.

pianissimo (pp) Very soft (*ppp* indicates a still softer dynamic).

piano (p) Soft.

più More.

pizzicato (*pizz.*) The string plucked with the finger.

plötzlich Suddenly, immediately.

plus More.

pochissimo (*pochiss.*) Very little, a very little.

poco Little, a little.

polychoral Polyphonic style developed in the late sixteenth century involving two or more choirs that alternate or sing together.

ponticello (*pont.*) The bridge (of a string instrument).

portamento Continuous smooth and rapid sliding between two pitches.

position naturel (*pos. nat.*) In the normal position (usually canceling an instruction to play using some special technique).

possibile Possible.

premier mouvement (*1er mouvt.*) At the original tempo.

prenez Take up.

préparez Prepare.

presque Almost, nearly.

presser To press.

prestissimo A more forceful indication of presto.

presto A very quick tempo (faster than *allegro*).

prima, primo First, principal.

quarta Fourth.

quasi Almost, as if.

quinto Fifth.

rallentando (*rall., rallent.*) Growing slower.

rapidamente Quickly.

rapidissimo (*rapidiss.*) Very quickly.

rasch Quickly.

rascher More quickly.

rauschend Rustling, roaring.

recitative (*recit.*) A vocal style designed to imitate and emphasize the natural inflections of speech.

refrain Text or music that is repeated within a larger composition, especially in a fixed poetic form such as the rondeau, virelai, or ballade.

rein Perfect interval.

repetizione Repetition.

reprise Repeat; in French Baroque music, the second section of a binary form.

Requiem Mass Roman Catholic Mass for the dead.

respiro Pause for breath.

retenu Held back.

r.h. Abbreviation for "right hand."

richtig Correct (*richtige Lage*, correct pitch).

rien Nothing.

rigore di tempo Strictness of tempo.

rinforzando (*rf., rfz., rinf.*) A sudden accent on a single note or chord.

ripieno Tutti; in a Baroque concerto grosso, the whole ensemble.

ritardando (*rit., ritard.*) Gradually slackening in speed.

ritenuto (*riten.*) Immediate reduction of speed.

ritmato Rhythmic.

ritornando, ritornello (*ritor.*) Refrain.

ronde Lively Renaissance "round dance," associated with the outdoors, in which the participants dance in a circle or a line.

rondeau Medieval or Renaissance fixed poetic form and chanson type with courtly love texts; also a French Baroque refrain form; related to the *rondo*.

rondo Musical form in which the first section recurs, usually in the tonic.

In the Classical multimovement cycle, is appears as the last movement in various forms, including **A-B-A-B-A, A-B-A-C-A,** and **A-B-A-C-A-B-A.**

rounded binary Compositional form with two sections, in which the second ends with a return to material from the first; each section is usually repeated.

rubato A certain elasticity and flexibility of tempo, consisting of slight accelerandos and ritardandos according to the requirements of the musical expression.

Rückpositiv Secondary division of an organ, with pipes behind the player.

ruhig Quietly.

sans Without.

Schalltrichter Horn.

scherzando (*scherz.*) Playful.

scherzo and trio composition in **A-B-A** form, usually in triple meter; replaced the minuet and trio.

schlagen To strike in a usual manner.

Schlagwerk Striking mechanism.

schleppen, schleppend Dragging.

Schluss Cadence, conclusion.

schnell Fast.

schneller Faster.

schon Already.

Schwammschlägeln Sponge-headed drumstick.

scorrevole Flowing, gliding.

sec, secco Dry, simple.

secundà Second.

segue Following immediately.

sehr Very.

semplicità Simplicity.

sempre Always, continually.

senza Without.

sequence A Medieval addition to the liturgy, sung after the Alleluia of the Mass.

serenade Classical instrumental genre that combines elements of chamber music and symphony, often performed in the evening or at social functions.

sesquialtera Organ stop of two ranks, which sounds the twelfth and the seventeenth.

seul Alone, solo.

scherzo Composition in **A-B-A** form, usually in triple meter; replaced the minuet and trio in the nineteenth century.

sforzando (*sf.*, *sfz.*) With sudden emphasis.

simile (*sim.*) In a similar manner.

sin Without.

sinfonia Short instrumental work, found in Baroque opera, to facilitate scene changes.

Singstimme Singing voice.

sino al Up to the . . . (usually followed by a new tempo marking, or by a dotted line indicating a terminal point).

si piace Especially pleasing.

smorzando (*smorz.*) Dying away.

sofort Immediately.

soli, solo (*s.*) Executed by one performer.

sonata Instrumental genre in several movements for soloist, duo, or small chamber ensemble.

sonata-allegro form The opening movement of the multimovement cycle, consisting of themes that are stated in the first section (exposition), developed in the second section (development), and restated in the third section (recapitulation).

sonata da camera Baroque instrumental work comprised of a series of dance movements.

sonata da chiesa Baroque instrumental work intended for performance in church; in four movements, frequently arranged slow-fast-slow-fast.

sopra Above; in piano music, used to indicate that one hand must pass above the other.

soprano (*S.*) The voice classification with the highest range.

sordini, sordino (*sord.*) Mute' soft pedal on piano.

sostenendo, sostenuto (*sost.*) Sustained.

sotto voce In an undertone, subdued, under the breath.

sourdine (*sourd.*) Mute.

soutenu Sustained.

spiel, spielen Play (an instrument).

Spieler Player, performer.

spirito Spirit, soul.

spiritoso In a spirited manner.

spugna Sponge.

staccato (*stacc.*) Detached, separated, abruptly, disconnected.

stentando, stentare, stentato (*stent.*) Delaying, retarding.

stesso The same.

stile concitato Agitated style, devised by Monteverdi, involving rapid reiterations of a single pitch.

Stimme Voice.

stimmen To tune.

strappato Bowing indication for pulled, or long, strokes.

strascinare To drag.

Streichinstrumente (*Streichinstr.*) Bowed string instruments.

strepitoso Noisy, loud.

stretto In a nonfugal composition, indicates a concluding section at an increased speed.

stringendo (*string.*) Quickening.

string quartet A multimovement composition for two violins, viola, and cello.

strophic form Song structure in which the same music is repeated with every stanza (strophe) of the poem.

subito (*sub.*) Suddenly, immediately.

suite A multimovement work made up of a series of contrasting dance movements, generally all in the same key.

sul On the (as in *sul G*, on the G string).

superius In older music, the uppermost part.

sur On.

symphony Large work for orchestra, generally in four movements.

tacet The instrument or vocal part so marked is silent.

tasto solo In a continuo part, this indicates that only the string instrument plays; the chord-playing instrument is silent.

tempo primo (*tempo I*) At the original tempo.

teneramente, tenero Tenderly, gently.

tenor, tenore (*T.*) The highest male voice; the structural voice in early music.

tenuto (*ten., tenu.*) Held, sustained.

ternary form Three-part (**A-B-A**) form.

tertia Third.

terzetto Vocal trio, often found in opera.

theme and variations Compositional procedure in which a theme is stated and then altered in successive statements.

tief Deep, low.

touche Key; note.

toujours Always, continually.

tranquillo Quietly, calmly.

tre corde (*t.c.*) Release the soft (or *una corda*) pedal of the piano.

tremolo (*trem.*) On string instruments, a quick reiteration of the same tone, produced by a rapid up-and-down movement of the bow; also a rapid alternation between two different notes.

très Very.

trill (*tr.*) The rapid alternation of a given note with the diatonic second above it. In a drum part, it indicates rapid alternating strokes with two drumsticks.

trio sonata Baroque chamber sonata type written in three parts: two melody lines and the *basso continuo*; requires a total of four players to perform.

Trommschlag (*Tromm.*) Drumbeat.

troppo Too much.

tutta la forza Very emphatically.

tutti Literally, "all"; usually means all the instruments in a given category as distinct from a solo part.

übergreifen To overlap.

übertonend Drowning out.

umstimmen To change the tuning.

un One, a.

una corda (*u.c.*) With the "soft" pedal of the piano depressed.

und And.

unison (*unis.*) The same notes or melody played by several instruments at the same pitch. Often used to emphasize that a phrase is not to be divided among several players.

unmerklich Imperceptible.

velocissimo Very swiftly.

verklingen lassen To let die away.

verse A group of lines in a poem, sometimes separated by a recurring refrain; also small units of text from the Bible, sung as a solo in alternation with a choral response.

vibrare To sound.

vibrato (*vibr.*) To fluctuate the pitch on a single note.

vierfach Quadruple.

vierhändig Four-hand piano music.

vif Lively.

vigoroso Vigorous, strong.

vivace Quick, lively.

vivacissimo A more forceful indication of *vivace*.

vivente, vivo Lively.

voce Voice (as in *colla voce*, a direction for the accompaniment to follow the solo part in tempo and expression).

volles orch. Entire orchestra.

Vorhang auf Curtain up.

Vorhang zu Curtain down.

vorher Beforehand, previously.

voriges Preceding.

Waltzertempo In the tempo of a waltz.

weg Away, beyond.

weich Mellow, smooth, soft.

wie aus der Fern As if from afar.

wieder Again.

wie zu Anfang dieser Szene As at the beginning of this scene.

zart Tenderly, delicately.

Zeit Time; duration.

zögernd Slower.

zu The phrases *zu 2, zu 3* (etc.) indicate the number of parts to be played by 2, 3 (etc.) players.

zum In addition.

zurückhaltend Slackening in speed.

zurücktreten To withdraw.

zweihändig With two hands.

Appendix D
*Concordance Table for Recordings
and Listening Guides*

The following table provides cross-references to the Listening Guides (LG) in *The Enjoyment of Music*, Tenth Edition, by Kristine Forney and Joseph Machlis (New York: W. W. Norton, 2007). The table also gives the track numbers for each work on both recording sets (see "A Note on the Recordings," p. xiv).

LG #	Shorter LG #	Score Number, Composer, Title	Score Page	8-CD Set	4-CD Set
1	1	BRITTEN: *Young Person's Guide to the Orchestra*	—	(Student Resource CD)	(Student Resource CD)
2		1. GREGORIAN CHANT: Kyrie	1	1 (1–3)	—
3	2	2. HILDEGARD VON BINGEN: *Alleluia, O virga mediatrix*	3	1 (4–6)	1 (1–3)
4	3	3. NOTRE DAME SCHOOL ORGANUM: *Gaude Maria virgo*	8	1 (7–8)	1 (4–5)
5		4. ANONYMOUS: *Mout me fu grief/ Robin m'aime/Portare*	10	1 (9–10)	—
6	4	5. RAIMBAUT DE VAQUEIRAS: *Kalenda maya*	13	1 (11–15)	1 (6–10)
7	5	6. MACHAUT: *Puis qu'en oubli*	17	1 (16–20)	1 (11–15)
8		7. DU FAY: *L'homme armé* Mass, Kyrie	19	1 (21–24)	—
9	6	8. JOSQUIN: *Ave Maria . . . virgo serena*	26	1 (25–31)	1 (16–22)
10	7	9. PALESTRINA: *Pope Marcellus* Mass, Gloria	35	1 (32–33)	1 (23–24)
15		10. GABRIELI: *O quam suavis*	43	1 (34–35)	—
11		11. JOSQUIN: *Mille regretz*	53	1 (36–37)	—
12	8	12. SUSATO: Three Dances	56	1 (38–41)	1 (25–28)
13	9	13. MONTEVERDI: *Ecco mormorar l'onde*	60	1 (42–44)	1 (29–31)
14	10	14. FARMER: *Fair Phyllis*	69	1 (45–46)	1 (32–33)

LG #	Shorter LG #	Score Number, Composer, Title	Score Page	8-CD Set	4-CD Set
16		15. MONTEVERDI: *L'incoronazione di Poppea*, Act III, Finale	74	1 (47–51)	—
17	11	16. PURCELL: *Dido and Aeneas*, Act III			
		Dido's Lament	84	1 (52–54)	1 (34–36)
		Chorus		1 (55)	—
18		17. HANDEL: *Rinaldo*, "Molto voglio"	91	1 (56–58)	—
29		18. GAY: *The Beggar's Opera*, end of Act II	96	1 (59–61)	—
19	12	19. STROZZI: *Begli occhi*		1 (62–67)	1 (37–42)
20	13	20. BACH: Cantata No. 80, *Ein feste Burg ist unser Gott*			
		No. 1. Choral fugue	109	2 (1–7)	1 (43–49)
		No. 2. Duet	136	2 (8–9)	—
		No. 5. Chorus	144	2 (10–11)	—
		No. 8. Chorale	162	2 (12–13)	1 (50–51)
21	14	21. HANDEL: *Messiah*			
		No. 1. (Overture)	165	2 (14–15)	—
		No. 14. "There were shepherds"	171	2 (16–18)	—
		No. 17. "Glory to God"	173	2 (19)	—
		No. 18. "Rejoice greatly"	178	2 (20–22)	1 (52–54)
		No. 44. "Hallelujah"	184	2 (23–25)	1 (55–57)
22		22. CORELLI: Trio Sonata, Op. 3, No. 2, in D major			
		Third movement	195	2 (26)	—
		Fourth movement	196	2 (27–28)	—
23		23. SCARLATTI: Sonata in C major, K. 159 (*La Caccia*)	199	2 (29–30)	—
28	18	24. BACH: Contrapunctus I, from *The Art of Fugue*	203	2 (31–34)	1 (58–61)
24	15	25. VIVALDI: *La primavera*, from *Le quattro stagioni*			
		First movement	208	2 (35–40)	1 (62–67)
		Second movement	219	2 (41)	—
		Third movement	223	2 (42)	—
25		26. BACH: *Brandenburg Concerto* No 2 in F major, first movement	238	2 (43–47)	—
26	16	27. HANDEL: *Water Music*, Suite in D major			
		Allegro	259	2 (48–50)	—
		Alla hornpipe	264	2 (51–53)	2 (1–3)
27	17	28. MOURET: Rondeau, from *Suite de symphonies*	271	2 (54–56)	1 (68–70)
30		29. HAYDN: String Quartet in D minor, Op 76, No. 2 (*Quinten*), fourth movement	275	2 (57–62)	—
31	19	30. MOZART: *Eine kleine Nachtmusik*, K. 525			
		First movement	284	3 (1–5)	1 (71–75)
		Second movement	291	3 (6–11)	—
		Third movement	296	3 (12–14)	1 (76–78)
		Fourth movement	297	3 (15–20)	—
32		31. MOZART: Symphony No. 40 in, G minor K. 550, first movement	307	3 (21–25)	—

(*Continued*)

LG #	Shorter LG #	Score Number, Composer, Title	Score Page	8-CD Set	4-CD Set
33	20	32. HAYDN: Symphony No. 94 in G major (*Surprise*), second movement	334	3 (26–32)	1 (79–85)
34	21	33. BEETHOVEN: Symphony No. 5 in C minor, Op. 67			
		First movement	347	3 (33–38)	2 (4–9)
		Second movement	363	3 (39–45)	2 (10–16)
		Third movement	378	3 (46–49)	2 (17–20)
		Fourth movement	390	3 (50–57)	2 (21–28)
35	22	34. MOZART: Piano Concerto in G major, K. 453			
		First movement	435	4 (1–11)	2 (29–39)
		Second movement	467	4 (12–17)	—
		Third movement	478	4 (18–24)	—
36		35. HAYDN: Trumpet Concerto in E-flat major, third movement	504	4 (25–30)	—
37		36. MOZART: Piano Sonata in A major, K. 331, third movement	521	4 (31–37)	—
38	23	37. BEETHOVEN: Piano Sonata in C-sharp minor, Op. 27, No. 2 (*Moonlight*)			
		First movement	526	4 (38–41)	2 (40–43)
		Second movement	529	4 (42–46)	2 (44–48)
		Third movement	529	4 (47–51)	—
39		38. MOZART: *Requiem*			
		Dies irae	539	4 (52–53)	—
		Tuba mirum	544	4 (54–58)	—
		Rex tremendae	549	4 (59)	—
40		39. HAYDN: *Die Schöpfung*, Part I, Nos. 12–14	554	3 (58–60)	—
41	24	40. MOZART: *Le nozze di Figaro*			
		Overture	571	4 (60–64)	—
		Act I, Scenes 6 and 7	593	4 (65–72)	2 (49–56)

Credits

p. 1 Gregorian Chant: Kyrie, from the *Liber usualis*. Used by permission of St. Bonaventure Publications. **p. 3 Hildegard von Bingen:** *Alleluia, O virgo mediatrix*. Lieder. Nach den Handschriften herausgegeben v. Pudentiana Barth OSB und Joseph Schmidt-Görg. © Otto Muller Verlag, 2. Auflage, Salzburg 1992. Reprinted by permission. Transcription reprinted by permission of Carl Fischer, LLC. **p. 8 Anonymous:** *Gaude Maria virgo* from *Le Magnus Liber Organi de Notre-Dame de Paris, Volume 1: Les Quadrupla et Tripla de Paris*. Ed. Edward H. Roesner. © Copyright Editions de l'Oiseau-lyre S.A.M., Monaco, 1993. Used by permission. **p. 10 Anonymous:** *Mout me fu grief/ Robin m'aime/Portrare*. Ed. Kristine Forney. **p. 13 Vaquieras:** *Kalenda maya* and translation from *Medieval Instrumental Dances*, ed. Timothy J. McGee, pp. 50–51. © Indiana University Press. Used by permission of Indiana University Press. **p. 17 Machaut:** *Puis qu'en oubli* from *Polyphonic Music of the Fourteenth Century*, Vol. III. Ed. Leo Schrade. © Copyright Editions de l'Oiseau-Lyre S.A.M., Monaco 1974. Used by permission. **p. 19 Du Fay:** *L'homme armé* Mass, Kyrie. Used by permission of Alejandro Planchart. **p. 26 Josquin:** *Ave Maria . . . virgo serena* from *Anthology of Renaissance Music*, ed. Allan Atlas. Used by permission of Alejandro Planchart. **p. 35 Palestrina:** *Pope Marcellus* Mass, Gloria from *Palestrina Opera Omnia*. Published by Fondazione Istituto Italiano per la Storia della Musica, Rome, Italy. Used by permission. **p. 43 Gabrieli:** *O quam suavis* from *Opera omina*, ed. Denis Arnold, CMM 12-1. © 1956, American Institute of Musicology. Used by permission. **p. 53 Josquin:** *Mille regretz* reprinted by permission of the publisher from *Chanson and Madrigal, 1480–1530: Studies in Comparison and Contrast*, A Conference at Isham Memorial Library. September 13–14, 1961, edited by James Haar, pp. 143–146, Cambridge, Mass.: Harvard University Press, Copyright © 1964 by the President and Fellows of Harvard College. **p. 56 Susato:** Three Dances (*Rondes*, published 1551). Ed. Kristine Forney.

Music, Suite in D major, Allegro and Alla hornpipe, from *Water Music and Music for The Royal Fireworks in Full Score*, New York, NY: Dover Publications, Inc. **p. 271 Mouret:** Rondeau, from *Suite de symphonies*. Ed. Kristine Forney. **p. 275 Haydn:** String Quartet in D minor, Op. 76, No. 2, Fourth movement. Used by kind permission of European American Music Distributors LLC, sole U. S. and Canadian agent for Ernst Eulenburg & Co GmbH. **p. 284 Mozart:** *Eine kleine Nachtmusik*, ed. Dieter Rexroth. © 1983 Ernst Eulenburg & Co GmbH. All Rights Reserved. Used by permission of European American Music Distributors LLC, sole U.S. and Canadian agent for Ernst Eulenburg & Co GmbH. **p. 307 Mozart:** Symphony No. 40 in G minor, K. 550, First movement. © 1983 Ernst Eulenburg Ltd. All Rights Reserved. Used by permission of European American Music Distributors LLC, sole U. S. and Canadian agent for Ernst Eulenburg & Co GmbH. **p. 334 Haydn:** Symphony No. 94 in G major (*Surprise*), Second movement. Ed. Harry Newstone. © 1984 Ernst Eulenburg Ltd. All Rights Reserved. Used by permission of European American Music Distributors LLC, sole U. S. and Canadian agent for Ernst Eulenburg & Co GmbH. **p. 347 Beethoven:** Symphony No. 5 in C minor, Op. 67, from *Symphonies Nos. 5, 6, and 7 in Full Scores*, New York, NY: Dover Publications, Inc. **p. 435 Mozart:** Piano Concerto in G major, K. 453, from the New Mozart Edition (BA 5384) (Eva and Paul Badura-Skoda). Reprinted by permission of Baerenreiter Music Corporation. **p. 504 Haydn:** Trumpet Concerto in E-flat major, Third movement. © 1991 by G. Henle Verlag, Munich. Used by permission. **p. 521 Mozart:** Piano Sonata in A major, K. 331, Third movement, from *Complete Sonatas and Fantasies for Solo Piano*. New York, NY: Dover Publications, Inc. **p. 526 Beethoven:** Piano Sonata No. 14 in C-sharp minor, Op. 27, No. 2 (*Moonlight*), from Kalmus Ur-text edition. **p. 539 Mozart:** Requiem, excerpts from Carus-Verlag edition. Copyright 1996/2004 by Carus-Verlag, Stuttgart, Germany. Reprinted by permission. **p. 554 Haydn:** *The Creation*. Arr. Vincent Novello. Copyright © 1951 (Renewed) by G. Schirmer, Inc. (ASCAP). International Copyright Secured. All Rights Reserved. Reprinted by Permission. **p. 571 Mozart:** *Le nozze di Figaro*, Overture. Used with kind permission of European American Music Distributors LLC, sole U. S. and Canadian agent for Ernst Eulenburg & Co GmbH. **p. 593 Mozart:** *Le nozze di Figaro*, Act I, Scenes 6 and 7. English translation by Ruth and Thomas Martin. Copyright © 1947, 1951 (Renewed) by G. Schirmer, Inc.(ASCAP). International Copyright Secured. All Rights Reserved. Reprinted by Permission.

Index of Forms and Genres

A roman numeral following a title indicates a movement within the work named.

The Norton
SCORES

Edited by Kristine Forney, with Textual Notes by Roger Hickman

VOLUME 1: GREGORIAN CHANT TO BEETHOVEN   TENTH EDITION

The Norton Scores, Tenth Edition, is a remarkable collection of works from the Middle Ages to the present. In addition to many familiar pieces, this new edition includes selections from musical theater, jazz, and traditional music; compositions by women; contemporary and electronic compositions; and works from traditional, popular, and non-Western styles. This volume also features:

- a unique highlighting system—long a standard of this anthology— that makes it easy to follow a full orchestral score

- stylistic and contextual commentary for each piece

- discussion of performance practice issues

- scores from excellent editions, some newly typeset for readability

- English translations for all foreign-language vocal works

- CD track numbers throughout each score for both sets of *The Norton Recordings*

- three appendices: *Reading a Musical Score* (with instrument transpositions) and *Instrumental Names and Abbreviations;* a *Glossary;* and a *Concordance Table* cross-referencing the scores with the Listening Guides in both versions of *The Enjoyment of Music* and track numbers for both CD sets

- a complete *Index of Forms and Genres*

The Norton Scores are paired with *The Norton Recordings*, an 8-CD set in two volumes including every work found in this anthology, and *The Norton Recordings, Shorter,* a 4-CD set containing a selection of pieces from both volumes of the scores.

Cover design: Antonina Krass
Cover art: *Composition II, 1996,* by Roy Lichtenstein. © Estate of Roy Lichtenstein.

ISBN-13: 978-0-393-92889-1
ISBN-10: 0-393-92889-6

W. W. NORTON New York · London
www.wwnorton.com

9 780393 928891